Dear Reader,

I'm so thrilled you could join me on a visit to Mary and the wonderful folks at Ivy Bay! I was especially excited to write about Living History Day and all the wonderful demonstrations the townsfolk were up to.

When I was in high school, one of my mother's friends went to Thailand and brought back a gift for me—a handmade book with colored pages and handmade paper decorating the cover boards. I absolutely loved this book and the unique feel of the homemade paper, as well as the unique construction of the book, which appeared different from other hardcover books I'd seen.

At first I was reluctant to use it, but I ended up writing prayer requests in that book for many years until it was filled. I loved taking it out and feeling the soft pages as I prayed over the requests written in it.

For Mary's demonstration on bookbinding, the research was a joy as I learned how books are made. And then it was my little handmade book I thought of as I wrote about Mary painstakingly creating a book from scratch.

It is my hope that this book both entertains and delights your soul as you read.

In Christ,
Camy Tang

Secrets of Mary's Bookshop

A Classic Case

SECRETS *of* MARY'S
BOOKSHOP

A Classic Case

Camy Tang

Guideposts

New York

Secrets of Mary's Bookshop is a trademark of Guideposts.

Published by Guideposts
16 E. 34th St.
New York, NY 10016
Guideposts.org

Acknowledgments

Every attempt has been made to credit the sources of copyrighted material used in this book. If any such acknowledgment has been inadvertently omitted or miscredited, receipt of such information would be appreciated.

"From the Guideposts Archives" originally appeared in *Daily Guideposts 2006*. Copyright © 2005 by Guideposts. All rights reserved.

Cover and interior design by Müllerhaus
Cover illustration by Ross Jones at Deborah Wolfe, Ltd.
Typeset by Aptara, Inc.

Printed and bound in the United States of America
10 9 8 7 6 5 4 3 2 1

A Classic Case

ONE

The bright morning sun made the cold autumn air seem to sparkle as Mary Fisher headed to open up her bookshop. Today was Living History Day in Ivy Bay, and the weather couldn't have cooperated better. The light brightened the red, gold, and nutmeg colors of the leaves on the trees, and the cranberry bog behind the house was such a bright scarlet it almost hurt her eyes to look at it. She whispered a quick prayer of thanks to God for leading her back to Ivy Bay, where she and her sister had spent so many happy summers. She'd moved in with Betty shortly after her husband, John, had passed away, and soon after that, she'd opened her dream business, Mary's Mystery Bookshop. She thanked God for the blessing of new beginnings.

Mary's widowed sister Betty had already left earlier that morning to help out with the living history event. Betty and her sister-in-law Eleanor were deeply involved in the planning of this fun day where the shops along downtown Ivy Bay would feature demonstrations on how people lived in the past.

On her way to her shop, Mary did a double take when she saw Johanna Montgomery, the head reporter for the

Ivy Bay Bugle, dressed in a black Victorian dress with white at the collar and cuffs. She grinned when she saw Mary and crossed the street to her.

"You look fantastic," Mary said. "Where did you get that dress?"

"I made it." Johanna proudly ran a hand down the black fabric of her full skirt. "I found a pattern for a reproduction dress and spent a few weeks making it. I chose a simple pattern on purpose"—she winked—"so it wasn't as hard as I thought it would be."

"You even did a Victorian hairdo." Mary marveled at Johanna's highlighted brown hair swept up at the back of her head in a mass of braids.

Johanna carefully touched the do. "That was trickier than making the dress."

"Well, it looks great."

"Let's hope that antique printing press doesn't leak all over me and ruin my costume. I did a dry run last night and got ink all over my hands."

"I'm sure people in the 1800s got ink on their hands when they printed newspapers with movable type."

"At least it'll be fun to show everyone how it was done. This Living History Day is such a great idea."

At that moment, they saw Dr. Gary Teagarden across the street, heading to his office. Like Johanna, he was dressed in Victorian costume. He smiled and tipped his black top hat to them as he swung his cane jauntily. Mary and Johanna waved to him as he sailed by, the long tails of his black coat flapping behind him.

"What will Dr. Teagarden be doing?" Johanna asked Mary.

"I read in the schedule that he's giving a tour of his offices, which were built in the mid-nineteenth century, from what I remember."

"I hope I'll be able to make it for a tour after my demonstration. What are you doing?"

"I'll be demonstrating bookbinding."

"How neat!"

"Speaking of my store"—Mary checked her watch—"I need to get there."

"I need to get to the newspaper office too. See you later!"

As Mary approached her shop and Sweet Susan's Bakery next door, the warm smell of cinnamon, sugar, and other baked goodies grew stronger. Mary's employee Rebecca and her daughter Ashley had just walked up to the front door of her bookstore.

"Good morning!" Ashley said. Her exuberance made Mary's smile widen even more, and she gave the little girl a hug.

"Good morning," Rebecca said to Mary. "It's going to be a great day for Living History Day."

"I'm so pleased. The weather report was dead-on." Mary unlocked the front door and let them into the shop. Even though she'd had the shop for quite some time now, she was always pleasantly struck by the smell of books and paper when she first opened the front door in the mornings. The smell was like a handshake from an old friend.

"No Gus today?" Ashley asked, referring to Mary's gray cat, which usually came with Mary to the store in the morning in his carrier.

"I decided not to bring him. We'll have quite a few people because of the events happening at the shops along the street today."

"He won't run away, will he?" Ashley looked surprised.

"No, but there might be a lot to startle him."

Ashley grinned, looking younger than her seven years old. "Aw, I would have protected Gus from the big, bad customers."

Mary laughed.

"Since Gus isn't here for me to protect, what else can I do to help?"

"Could you set out the cups? I'm sure several people will want tea and coffee, despite the sunshine."

As Ashley headed to the back of the store, Rebecca asked, "When did you want to set up for the bookbinding demonstration?"

"We can set up on the sidewalk now. The sight of the bookbinding apparatus might get people even more curious to see the demonstration."

As they were setting up, Rebecca asked, "Would it be all right if we closed the shop at noon during the robbery reenactment at the bank so that Ashley and I could go? Unless you weren't planning to go—"

"I most definitely was going to go. I actually lent Steve the book on an original historic robbery that took place at the bank, and it gave him the idea to do the reenactment."

"I can't imagine Ivy Bay Bank & Trust ever being held up by robbers. It looks so imposing."

"Well, I haven't read the book, but the cover has a drawing of the bank as it was in 1870 when it was robbed, and it was only a small wooden building, not very imposing at all."

As they bustled back and forth between the store and the sidewalk to finish setting things up for Living History Day, Mary took a moment to look out the window. Meeting House Grocers always opened early, but right now, the employees were hustling around, getting ready to sell some old-fashioned caramel apples, with the owner Jeremy Court dressed up in an old-fashioned apron and his wife, Kaley, in a Victorian shopgirl's dress. Next door was Gems and Antiques, and while Mary couldn't see Jayne out front, there were already a couple of antique spinning wheels set up in front of the store.

Mary also saw the figure of Owen Cooper, the president of the bank, heading inside the brick building. He had the uncharacteristically grim look on his face that he'd been carrying for the past several weeks, possibly to do with the rumors about Ivy Bay Bank & Trust.

Rebecca followed Mary's gaze and saw Owen also. "Do you think the rumors are true? That the bank will close?"

"I certainly hope not."

"But he's your neighbor. You haven't asked him about it?"

Mary winced. "I haven't wanted to bother him about it, especially since he's looked so stressed lately."

"I heard that the Boston banking corporation that owns Ivy Bay Bank & Trust, the Neels Banking Group, is sending an accountant to look at the financials and see if it'll stay open or be closed down."

Mary nodded noncommittally, not sure how much she should say. A few days ago, while she and Betty were walking along the beach, they'd happened to meet up with their old friend Todd Milton, who owned the Beacon Inn. They'd fallen into discussing the news about how other banks owned by the Neels Banking Group had been shut down in the past few weeks because of cost cutting. Everyone was worried that Ivy Bay Bank & Trust would fall under the same hammer. Todd had said with a frown that the Neels Banking Group had reserved a room for someone to arrive in Ivy Bay tomorrow, and Mary and Betty suspected it was indeed an accountant or someone who would be looking over the bank records to determine if it would stay open or not.

"It would be terrible if the bank closed," Rebecca said to Mary. "Practically everyone in Ivy Bay banks there. It's such an important part of our community."

Mary agreed. "Sandra, Steve, and Owen always have smiles on their faces and ask how people are. They go out of their way to help their customers." Steve had been particularly helpful when Mary first started setting up her business and had advised her as to the best way to set up her banking for the shop. "Plus, there aren't many banks willing to contribute to a community event like Living History Day by holding a historical robbery reenactment, don't you think?"

Mary and Rebecca had arrived at the store early because a few of the events for Living History Day were scheduled to start at nine o'clock, and they wanted to be open when people came for the other demonstrations. It was only eight, but there were already people strolling along the sidewalks with the bright yellow-colored flyers in their hands. Jerry Avakian, who owned Meeting House Print and Copy, had printed the flyers, listing the schedule of events. All the shop owners downtown had helped distribute them in the past several weeks.

By the time nine o'clock rolled around, the streets were filled with people. Mary had one of the first demonstration time slots—the only earlier one was a demonstration on churning butter at Sweet Susan's Bakery next door, so Mary, Ashley, and Rebecca were able to watch Susan's demonstration before they started their own.

The bakery was crowded with people buying sweets even while Susan Crosby stood out on the sidewalk demonstrating butter making. She'd dressed in a simple dark dress and white apron and cap, looking like she'd stepped out of a historical novel. She churned butter in a wooden churn with a paddle and then also in a glass jar fitted with a special lid that had a paddle attachment.

"This glass butter churn belonged to my great-grandmother," Susan said to the crowd, and one or two people mentioned family members who owned one too.

After Susan finished her demonstration at twenty minutes past nine, Mary went back to her shop and began her bookbinding demonstration, although several of the children remained in front of Susan's shop, taking turns churning butter. She didn't blame them one bit.

Mary had known immediately that she wanted to demonstrate old-fashioned bookbinding as her contribution to the event, even though she hadn't known herself how it was done. She figured it'd be a great opportunity for her to learn, so she did extensive research online. She'd made several lopsided test books before she finally got the hang of things, and she still wasn't entirely proficient at what she was doing, but she had the basics covered at least.

Mary presented a stack of "signatures"—several sheets of folded paper—which she'd prepared beforehand. She showed how to clamp all the signatures together and draw lines for sewing. Then she punched holes in each of the signatures with a special awl. Some of the holes were a bit off center, but she didn't think it showed too badly. After waxing her thread, she sewed the signatures to the cloth tapes she was using to help hold the signatures together. Next, she demonstrated gluing the signatures together, then gluing them to the mull cloth that also held the signatures together. These two steps required drying time, so she'd done this earlier and had already-dried samples ready to continue the demonstration. She'd also already cut out the cover boards from pressed illustration board and showed how to sand the edges smooth.

She demonstrated how to headband the top and bottom edges of the spine, but since it was a process that took a bit of time, she did only a little of it and then switched to a sample she'd done earlier where she'd completed the headbanding.

She then attached the signatures to the cover board, and again switched to an already-dried sample for the next step of gluing the cover boards to the paper cover, which she'd precut. She then demonstrated gluing the "turnover"— tucking the loose ends of the paper cover over the edges of the cover board to the inside. She fumbled a bit but managed to get it done without too much trouble. Then she glued the first and last pages of the signatures to the cover boards to hide the mull cloth and tapes.

At the end, she saw she'd gone a little long in her presentation, but people didn't seem to mind. They clapped, and a few women asked questions about some of the tools she'd used, such as the bone folder and the awl.

"I love making things," one woman said. "I want to try this method to make blank books for gifts."

"That's a great idea," Mary said. "You can cover the book with cloth instead of paper, and there are lots of artisan papers you can buy today to use for the pages, to make the book extra special."

People wandered away, heading to the next demonstration, but several remained to enter the bookstore and peruse the shelves. Mary and Rebecca were busy for the next hour talking to customers and ringing up sales, while Rebecca's daughter Ashley was invaluable in making recommendations to the kids who were in the children's section of the store. At the end of the hour, there was a slight lull.

"If it's all right with you, I'd like to watch the demonstration at the newspaper office where they're showing how they printed newspapers with movable type," Rebecca said to Mary. "It's scheduled for two o'clock. And Ashley wanted a tour of Dr. Teagarden's building this afternoon too."

"That's perfectly fine," Mary said. "I actually want to go down to see the horse-drawn carriages."

"Where are they?"

"According to the schedule, they're setting up at the library around ten o'clock and they'll be there all day. Why don't I go wander around this morning, and then I'll mind the shop this afternoon while you see the demonstrations?"

Rebecca grinned. "Deal."

Mary headed out—the crowd of customers in the shop had slimmed to only a couple of people idly browsing the shelves. She first went to the library, where the parking lot had been transformed into a stable yard, complete with hay strewn on the asphalt and some temporary wooden fencing put up. Horses were hitched up to Victorian buggies, and frontier wagons took visitors on rides around the parking lot, while there were a few ponies set up in a far corner for the children to ride. A few historians chatted about some antique vehicles parked to one side, which were not hitched up to any horses, and answered questions and described how people traveled in the 1800s.

Mary found Henry, her old childhood friend, quickly enough. He was talking to an older gentleman standing near an antique car. It had an open carriage with leather-upholstered seats and large, slender wheels.

"Hi, Mary," Henry said when he saw her, giving her a quick side hug. "Do you know Giles Durant?"

"Hi, there." Mary shook the hand of the tall, slender man. "I'm Mary Fisher, of Mary's Mystery Bookshop."

He nodded and smiled, his snow-white hair bright in the autumn sunlight. "Giles Durant, all the way from Boston."

"Is this your car?" she asked.

"Yep, passed down from my great-grandfather."

Henry's eyes sparkled as he gestured to the car. "Isn't she a beauty? Giles was just telling me that the car was made in France in the late 1890s, but she has a German engine."

"I don't think I've ever seen a car this old," Mary said, impressed.

"My great-grandfather bought it new," Giles said. "He brought it with him when he came to America in the early

1900s, and it's been passed down from father to son ever since."

"Did you drive it from Boston?"

"Oh no," Giles said with a chuckle. "I'm afraid it's not in working order anymore. But when Henry told me about Living History Day and that there were only horse-drawn carriages, I offered to have the car transported down for the day so people could see what one of the first automobiles looked like. This was made years before Henry Ford's assembly-line technique that made cars more affordable."

"This is wonderful. Thanks for coming down and letting us see it. I'm surprised you don't have the car in a museum."

"I had some offers, but I prefer to keep her and show her for school demonstrations and museum tours. I like talking to people about her." Giles patted the car's wheel. "A collector would be able to tell that she's been massively refurbished and her parts replaced, so she's not as 'authentic' as some other cars from that era."

"She looks authentic to me. And it's so neat to see what an early car looked like. Henry must be talking your ear off." She grinned at him.

"I've enjoyed catching up with Henry," Giles said. "We've known each other for years through an antique-car club we belong to, but we don't get a chance to chat very often."

"Since Living History Day was limited to the nineteenth century, I couldn't bring my 1953 Chevy Bel Air convertible," Henry lamented. "But I wanted a motorcar represented, which was why I called Giles."

"Are you going to be here all day?" she asked Henry. "Or are there any demonstrations you're going to go to?"

"What are you planning to see?" Henry said with a wink.

"I want to see the robbery reenactment. I lent Steve a historical book about the original robbery that gave him the idea for the reenactment."

"I remember seeing that in the schedule. It sounded neat, but I think I'm scheduled to volunteer at a booth here around that time," Henry said with a touch of disappointment.

"That's too bad."

At that moment, two tourists came up to admire the car and started asking questions about it. The tourists were obviously car buffs, and both Henry and Giles began talking animatedly with them. Mary bid them good-bye and left them cheerfully talking about cars.

She consulted the schedule of events and found that Jayne Tucker, who owned Gems and Antiques with her husband, Rich, was due to give the spinning demonstration. Mary walked down Meeting House Road and then turned right onto Main Street.

There was already a large crowd around the antiques store, and Jayne was in a calico dress, white ruffled apron, and bonnet, looking like she'd stepped out of *Little House on the Prairie*. She sat at a very large spinning wheel made of a dark-brown wood, and she held a curious wooden shaft with a tuft of long white strands attached to it. She held a small hank in her hand, making it look as if she were holding a cloud.

Jayne began speaking to the crowd, explaining the parts of the wheel such as the orifice, bobbin, and flyer hooks. "This particular wheel has a treadle so the spinner can spin the wheel by pumping with his or her foot." Jayne demonstrated by giving the wheel a little push with her hand and then pressing up and down on the treadle, which kept the wheel spinning merrily. "Other antique wheels didn't have a treadle, and the spinner had to spin the wheel by hand. They probably had great arm muscles." The crowd laughed.

"People spun all kinds of fiber, including wool, cotton, and what I'm demonstrating today, flax. Flax fiber is extracted from the bast or skin of the stem of the flax plant. Then the flax can be spun into a strong linen cord that can be used for all kinds of things. People would spin a fine linen thread for linen clothing, or they would spin a thick linen cord to use to tie things up.

"Now for the spinning. You start off by attaching a leader string." She tugged at a cotton yarn she'd tied to the core of her bobbin and then threaded it through the hooks and the orifice of the wheel. "You then attach a bit of fiber to the end of the leader string and start your wheel." She pushed the wheel and pumped on the treadle with her foot, and as the wheel whirled around, her leader string began to twist like the stripes on a barber pole.

"The wheel causes the fibers to twist, which is what creates the yarn. As the yarn twists, I feed more of this flax fiber forward and let it twist on itself. This is called drafting." Jayne's deft fingers pulled small amounts of the delicate fibers from the airy hank in her hand toward the twisted yarn, and the fluff became yarn. The yarn wound around the bobbin, which spun as quickly as the wheel did. Soon, Jayne had used up all the flax fiber in her hand, and she pulled another soft hank from the wooden shaft.

The crowd was quite large, so Mary moved her petite frame toward the far side so she would be able to better see Jayne's spinning. She accidentally bumped into someone. "I'm sorry. Oh, hi, Bea."

Bea Winslow, the county clerk, beamed at Mary. "Hi, Mary. Trying to see? Us short people have to jostle for position."

"Just to warn you, I've got sharp elbows." Mary grinned.

"Well, I've got my granddaughter as bodyguard."

Mary then noticed the slender teen standing beside Bea. "Hi, Megan. How's school going?"

Megan adjusted the thick plastic frames of her glasses and tucked her fine, straight brown hair behind her ear. Streaks of blue ran through her bangs. She shrugged. "Oh, it's fine, thanks."

"It's fall break right now, isn't it?"

Megan simply nodded.

"It must be great to have the week off of school," Mary said. "My sister Betty said that fall break was one reason they could hold Living History Day on a Monday."

"Yeah, some of the demonstrations are interesting, I guess," Megan said.

Mary knew that Megan, only a freshman in high school, wrote the computer program that enabled Bea to enter handwritten records into a searchable database. Megan was normally a confident girl, but today it seemed like something was a little wrong. Mary tried to engage Megan in conversation.

"Are you in computer club in school this year?" Mary asked Megan.

Megan nodded, but her eyes dropped to the ground.

"Don't be shy, Meg." Bea nudged her granddaughter. "Nothing to be ashamed of in being smart."

A small smile formed on Megan's lips. "That's cuz you say it runs in the family, Grandma."

"Well, doesn't it?" Bea's eyes twinkled.

Mary said to Megan, "I know grandmas are partial, and I know I've told you this before, but the program you wrote for your grandma at the county clerk's office helped me out a lot. It was brilliant."

Megan's cheeks dimpled. "Thanks, Mrs. Fisher. It was cool helping Grandma on that."

"And I paid her with some sort of chip too," Bea added.

"It was a memory chip, Grandma. It helps my computer run tons faster. And I told you that you didn't have to, so you're not allowed to complain about it after the fact." Megan rolled her eyes, but a smile slipped through her careful teenage guard.

Mary's attention was caught by Jayne again as she held up the yarn she had just spun, which twisted on itself. "This is called a 'singles,' and you can see it's quite twisty. Many weavers will use this 'singles' to weave linen fabric. However, after you let it rest, you ply two singles with each other to get a two-ply yarn. Then you can wash and 'set the twist,' which relaxes the twist in the yarn, and it'll come out looking like this." Jayne held up a length of thick linen cord, white and silky looking. "Anyone want to try spinning?"

"Do you want to go to the ice-cream demonstration?" Bea asked her granddaughter.

"Sure," Megan said.

"Coming?" Bea asked Mary. "I hear Tess Bailey is going to make ice cream the old-fashioned way, with ice and salt in a wooden ice-cream churn."

"I remember doing that with my grandmother," Mary said. "That was a lot of work."

"Tess will probably ask for lots of volunteers who 'get' to help churn the ice cream." Bea winked.

"I'll catch up with you later."

"Okay, see you later, Mary."

"Bye, Mrs. Fisher."

Mary watched as Jayne helped a woman get started on the spinning wheel. The process was fascinating, and the action of the wooden wheel and the twisting of the fibers into yarn seemed comforting, somehow. With Jayne's gentle guidance, the woman slowly started to understand the combined rhythm of drafting the fibers and pedaling the wheel at the right speed. As the woman started getting the hang of it, Jayne stepped back to watch her.

"You're so good at teaching spinning," Mary said to Jayne.

"I love it," Jayne said. "The action is so soothing. And when I'm spinning on an antique wheel, I feel connected to all the women who used that wheel before me."

But there was a sad light in Jayne's eyes even as she talked with pleasure about spinning. It reminded Mary of how down Jayne had seemed over the past week whenever she'd seen her. The first time, a week ago, Mary thought Jayne had simply had a bad day, but then she'd seen Jayne around downtown Ivy Bay a couple of times since then, and Jayne had still had that slightly anxious expression. Before, Mary had hesitated to ask Jayne if everything was all right, but she cared a great deal for Jayne, and her preoccupation worried Mary.

She had wondered if it had to do with Jayne's missing funds. Two weeks ago, Jayne had deposited some checks, but then had discovered they were never put into her account and the money was missing. Mary had been in the bank when Jayne came in to speak to Steve to find out what happened to her money, so she'd overheard their rather heated conversation. Steve promised to look into it and find the money, but Jayne had been particularly upset when she left.

However, Jayne's anxiety had been more pronounced this past week, as if it had been triggered by something besides the missing money. Mary stepped closer to Jayne and asked in a low, gentle voice, "How are you doing? Did the bank find your deposit yet?"

Jayne started slightly when Mary spoke to her, but answered calmly, "No, they haven't found it."

"Oh, that's terrible. You must be pretty upset. At least you seemed a bit down this past week."

Jayne hesitated, then gave Mary an overly bright smile. "No, I'm fine, really. I know the bank will find my money."

Mary felt a bit awkward and unsure how to respond. "I'm glad you're okay. If there's anything I can do, just let me know."

"That's sweet of you, Mary, but really, I'm fine. There's nothing wrong." Jayne turned slightly away from her.

Mary didn't press. She hoped it wasn't anything serious that was bothering Jayne. Or maybe she was mistaken about the anxiety she thought she'd seen in Jayne's face—maybe it did have to do with her funds and not something else.

Mary wandered off to Bailey's Ice Cream Shop and took a turn churning the ice cream in the wooden ice-cream churn, which was almost buried in a vat filled with ice sprinkled with coarse salt. Her arms ached after only a few minutes, and she was huffing and puffing.

"Sorry, Mary, you came at the tail end of this," Tess Bailey said. "The ice cream's harder to stir now because it's getting thick."

"It feels almost like taffy," Mary said, rubbing her arm as she relinquished the churn to an eager high-school boy.

But the ice cream tasted delicious. Tess had done a simple vanilla, but there were so many people that everyone only got a spoonful each. It tasted a bit different from the ice cream she made at home. The consistency of the ice cream was a little thicker, with the cream smooth against her tongue, and the taste of the vanilla beans was strong and almost flowery. It also seemed a little colder than ice cream she tasted out of her maker. Even though it was nearly lunchtime, several people opted to buy a scoop of ice cream from the shop, their appetites whetted by the ice-cream-churning demonstration.

"Oh no!"

Mary recognized the dismayed voice and turned to see Kaley Court holding her dog leash—with no dog attached. The young woman and her husband, Jeremy, were twisting around looking at the ground all around them, and it wasn't hard to guess that their golden retriever puppy Pipp had escaped.

Mary went up to them. "When did Pipp get loose?"

"I have no idea." Kaley's brown eyes fastened upon Mary. "We were watching the demonstration. He wriggled clean out of his collar, so he doesn't have any ID on him."

"He can't have gone far. I'll help you look for him."

"Thanks, Mary. If you look on the other side of the street, I'll look on this side, and Jeremy will run to the beach. Sometimes Pipp likes to run around the dunes."

Mary headed down Main Street, away from the beach, calling for Pipp. On the other side, Kaley wasn't quite keeping pace with her because her Victorian shopgirl dress tangled in her legs.

They'd reached the end of the street, and Kaley headed into her and Jeremy's store, Meeting House Grocers. Mary prepared to turn the corner when she thought she saw a wagging tail disappear behind the bank.

"Pipp!" Hurrying across Meeting House Road, Mary slipped down the narrow alley between Ivy Bay Bank & Trust and the frame shop next door. She was about to call Pipp's name again when she realized there were two men talking behind the bank.

No, not talking. One of them was yelling.

"If you weren't being so stubborn about the money...!"

At that moment, Mary caught sight of the dog and called, "Pipp! Come here!" The angry man's voice broke off abruptly.

Pipp disappeared around the corner of the bank, and Mary hurried after him, although a shiver of apprehension ran through her at the memory of that upset voice. She hoped she wasn't interrupting anything urgent.

She turned the corner to see Jerry Avakian towering over Steve Althorpe, the lead banker of Ivy Bay Bank & Trust. Jerry's olive skin had turned faintly purple, and his eyes blazed as he turned from Steve to frown at Mary and Pipp. Steve's face was impassive but pale.

"I'm sorry," Mary said breathlessly. "Pipp got away from the Courts, and I was trying to get him back." As she spoke, she reached out and snatched Pipp before he could scamper any farther away.

"It's fine, Mary," Steve said in a strained voice. "We're done. I need to change for the reenactment right now anyway."

Jerry opened his mouth as if to protest, but then he glanced at Mary and kept silent. Only when he relaxed his shoulders and stepped away from Steve did Mary realize how aggressive his stance had been. He seemed to be bullying Steve, who was slighter in build and shorter. The entire situation made her uncomfortable, and she tightened her grip on the impudent dog that had led her here.

"I've been looking forward to the robbery reenactment, Steve." Mary tried to make her voice light and natural. "I'll see you in a few minutes." She nodded to them both and hurried away back down the narrow alley and onto the street.

What had that been about? Why had they been behind the bank? Why had Jerry looked so belligerent and overbearing, and was that why Steve had looked a bit alarmed?

Mary didn't know Jerry well—he was a friend of Henry's, and he had always been hearty in his hellos when he saw her. She'd never before seen him look so angry and so threatening.

What had she just walked into?

———

Mary locked up her bookstore, and then she, Rebecca, and Ashley headed across the street to the bank, where people were streaming in through the open front doors for the robbery reenactment.

Ashley danced in excitement. "Do you think Mr. Althorpe will fire his gun?"

"I hope not," Rebecca said. "Even a blank gun would be deafening with all those high ceilings in the bank."

Ashley's face fell. "What's a bank robbery without shots fired?"

"Since when did you get so bloodthirsty?" Rebecca said, and Ashley giggled.

They entered Ivy Bay Bank & Trust and made their way along the perimeter of the room toward the front. The teller Sandra Rink was standing at her normal station behind the counter, and Mary went to stand in front of her.

"How are you doing, Sandra?" Mary asked.

"Oh, fine, Mrs. Fisher." Sandra flashed a quick smile, showing the cute gap between her front teeth. She wasn't dressed in costume, but rather than her normal conservative style, she'd put on a frilly cotton dress that looked faintly Victorian and she wore lovely pearl-and-gold earrings to match. Mary recognized the jewelry designer as a local artisan who made unique pieces—Mary had bought some earrings as gifts for friends in the past. But despite her more festive garb, Sandra's eyes were dark and somber today.

"I've been so worried after reading in the news about the Neels Banking Group closing down so many of its banks. Have you heard anything about Ivy Bay Bank & Trust?"

Sandra bit her lip. "I did, but I'm not supposed to talk about it."

"Oh, of course. But I am praying for all of you. Ivy Bay wouldn't be the same without this bank."

Sandra sighed. "I love working here in Ivy Bay, but . . . well, no one's job is secure at this point."

Sandra's low voice and the wrinkle between her brows made Mary even more concerned for the bank. It would be terrible if the bank closed.

But then she recalled Matthew chapter six, verses twenty-six and twenty-seven: *Look at the birds of the air; they do not sow or reap or store away in barns, and yet your heavenly Father feeds them. Are you not much more valuable than they? Can any one of you by worrying add a single hour to your life?*

Yes, she had to trust God.

"Miss Rink!" A chorus of excited voices rose above the murmur of conversation in the bank, and three teens came up to Sandra, who immediately grinned at them.

"I'm glad you guys made it," Sandra said to the girls, and Mary moved discreetly away. She wondered how the girls knew Sandra.

They obviously were close to the young woman, because one girl said, "I wish you'd been there to see Brittany collide with a cow!"

The girl who appeared to be Brittany rolled her eyes. "I didn't *collide* with the cow."

Sandra smiled and asked, "What happened?"

"I was at the cow-milking demonstration," Brittany said, "and the cow moved into *me*, not the other way around."

"Were you milking a cow?" Sandra asked with a laugh. "I wish I could've seen that."

"It was gigantic," one of the girls said.

"It kind of did a side step," Brittany said, "and then suddenly, I had a face full of cow!"

"She was on that little milking stool," one of the girls said, "so she went flying backward."

"I didn't go flying," Brittany protested, "but I did tip over kind of quickly."

All the girls giggled, and Mary had to smile, too, at the easy way they chatted with Sandra.

At that point, Owen Cooper, the president of the bank, raised his hand to get everyone's attention. "Thank you all for coming to our little reenactment. If you could all stand behind these taped lines on the floor, that'll ensure any would-be robbers don't accidentally shoot an innocent bystander." He chuckled, and several people laughed also as they shuffled behind the lines taped on the floor, leaving a stretch of empty space from the door to the small doorway leading to the back of the bank.

"Back in 1870, this bank was robbed by the dreaded thief Elias Cowper. He was the most notorious bank robber in this part of the country. He was apprehended three years after making off with the entire contents of the vault at Ivy Bay Bank. Now, back then, the bank was a lot smaller. In the 1950s, Ivy Bay Bank & Trust installed a new, modern vault, and the original vault was renovated to hold the safe-deposit boxes instead. We're making our reenactment today as authentic as possible, and the original vault is filled with the bank's 'money.'" Owen winked to let the crowd know that it wasn't real cash. "We hope you enjoy our little theatrics today."

Owen moved to stand behind the lead banker's desk, where Steve normally stood, and waited. And waited. The crowd shifted restlessly, and a slight frown appeared on Owen's face when suddenly a shadow fell across the light coming from the open bank door. Without warning, a deafening *bang* shot through the room, making Mary's ears ring.

"This is a holdup!" A man dressed in all black, with a hat pulled low over his forehead and a red bandanna tied around his nose and mouth, stood just outside the doorway to the bank. His voice was muffled by the bandanna, but it also sounded much gruffer than Steve's normal voice, making him seem actually dangerous. A nervous flutter went through Mary.

At first, her gut reaction was that this wasn't Steve. The height and build was about right, but something about the way he moved and spoke just wasn't Steve. But then she realized, that was the point, because he was in character. She was impressed at Steve's acting.

He strutted into the bank, waving his gun around. Even though the crowd knew it was all an act, several of those closest to the robber stepped back and ducked a little when the gun passed over them. However, when the robber took a menacing step toward them, most people gasped, then laughed. Many people held their cameras and cell phones up.

Mary hoped he wasn't going to fire the gun again. His first shot had been just outside the door rather than inside the bank, but it had still been incredibly loud. No wonder people froze when a robber said to "Stand and deliver!"

Mary noticed Jayne leaving the bank in the middle of the reenactment—maybe the sound had been too much for her.

"Open the vault!" Steve demanded from Owen, who did a credible job playing the cowed bank manager, his head down and his hands fluttering nervously. He disappeared behind the counter through the doorway with the robber following behind him, aiming the gun at him.

As the crowd was waiting for the robber to reappear, they were suddenly startled by two more shots fired, this time inside the safe-deposit vault. There was some nervous tittering. Mary glanced at Sandra, but she seemed as surprised as the rest of them. Perhaps Steve hadn't told her he was going to fire the gun inside the vault. Had that detail been in the historical book on the original bank robbery that Mary had lent to Steve? Now she wished she'd read it before passing it on to him.

The robber rushed out of the vault with a burlap sack heavy with his spoils. He waved the gun at the crowd before disappearing out the door.

The crowd laughed, and Mary smiled, waiting for Owen to reappear, but he seemed to be taking a long time. The crowd looked at one another, wondering what was supposed to happen next. Was the enactment over, or was there something else?

Sandra took a hesitant step, paused, then seemed to make a decision and strode toward the safe-deposit vault. Mary watched her and wondered if maybe Owen had been tied up by the robber. Steve had mentioned that he'd recreate the robbery as exactly as possible. If the manager had been tied up, Steve might have made sure to do that.

Suddenly, Sandra came running out of the vault. "Someone call the police! The bank's been robbed!"

TWO

·◆◆·

Some people froze at Sandra's announcement. Others laughed, thinking this was still part of the reenactment. Others seemed confused. Mary experienced a mix of the three.

But then Sandra shouted again, "This isn't part of the reenactment! The bank has really been robbed!"

Mary felt like her limbs had turned to stone. A real robbery? But Steve wouldn't do something like that! What had happened?

It was only when Owen came stumbling out of the vault, with a few streaks of red on his face, that people realized Sandra really was telling the truth. Sandra ran to Owen and grabbed some tissues from a box on a desk to press against his face.

Several people got out their cell phones to call the police, but since there were patrol cars throughout downtown to help with Living History Day, Deputy Wadell ran into the bank within a couple of minutes.

"What happened?" he asked to no one in particular.

Owen had been leaning heavily against the doorway to the vault, with Sandra beside him and trying to get him to a desk a few feet away to sit down. Now he gestured to the young officer, who hurried to him and helped support him to a chair.

"The robber took some safe-deposit boxes," Owen said weakly.

"Which ones?" demanded a strident female voice. Mary looked and recognized Judith Dougher.

Owen shook his head. "I don't know which ones. He hit me with his gun and tied me up, then shot at some of the boxes and took the contents. I couldn't see anything until Sandra came to untie me."

Deputy Wadell spoke low, terse words into the walkie-talkie at his shoulder, then turned back to Owen. "I've called the chief, and the paramedics are on their way. Just sit tight."

But Owen shook his head, his eyes wide. "You've got to stop him."

"I've put a call in for officers to look for a masked man, but he might have dropped the mask by now."

"He wasn't just any masked man, Deputy. It was Steve."

The accusation, coming from Owen's mouth, made it all suddenly terribly real to Mary. Ivy Bay Bank & Trust had been robbed! And it was Steve who'd done it! She couldn't believe it. Not Steve.

Sandra stood beside Owen, but her hands shook. The officer noticed and said, "Maybe you should sit down...."

"No, I'm fine," she said, although in a weak voice.

At that point, Rebecca and Ashley had moved through the crowd and found her. "Are you all right?" Mary asked them.

"We're fine," Ashley said, her eyes wide.

"I can't believe this," Rebecca said, putting her arm tight around Ashley.

Mary noticed that the crowd of people had started muttering to one another. Some people seemed bewildered; others seemed angry. A few people seemed a little excited that quiet Ivy Bay had something as unusual as a bank robbery. And in broad daylight too!

Some people started drifting out the front doors, and the deputy said, "Could you all please stay inside? At least until we can get your statements."

Most people grumbled, although Mary could understand why the police needed them to stay. She drew Rebecca and Ashley back to a relatively empty area near the windows.

The windows faced the side of the bank and the small parking lot, and Mary looked out. She looked hard at each of the cars there, but didn't see Steve's car in its normal spot, where she usually saw it every day.

It didn't take long for Chief McArthur to arrive with a few other officers. The chief talked to Owen in a low voice while some of the officers started taking reports from people in the crowd. Other officers went into the vault with what looked like fishing kits.

"What are they doing?" Ashley asked.

"I'm guessing they're going to take evidence and examine the crime scene," Mary said.

An officer came to the three of them to get their statements. Mary told what had happened as concisely as possible. He looked a little bored, and Mary guessed he'd listened to the same story told over and over by each person in the crowd in the bank.

"Okay, you can go," the officer told the three of them after getting their contact information. "We'll call you if we have any other questions."

"Thank you," Mary said and headed toward the door, Rebecca and Ashley ahead of her.

As she passed through the door, an officer ran into the bank, swiftly maneuvering around her, and she overheard him say to Chief McArthur, "We can't find Steve, sir."

"Anywhere?" The chief sounded annoyed and concerned at the same time.

Mary slowed her steps.

The officer said, "He's not at his house, but we have someone watching it right now. I went to the marina, but his boat is gone."

Everyone in Ivy Bay knew that Steve owned a nice boat that he used to sail down the coast with his parents when they were alive. They had cousins down in North Carolina, and Steve's boat was large enough for a prolonged sea voyage. Had Steve taken the valuables from the robbery and escaped in his boat? Mary had such a hard time believing it.

"Did anyone see him go?" Chief McArthur asked the officer.

"I questioned everyone there, but no one noticed Steve taking his boat out. It might have been right after the robbery, but no one remembers seeing it last night either. That clerk who works at Barnaby's smoke shop down by the docks remembers seeing it yesterday morning."

"Inform the coast guard to keep an eye out for it."

"Yes, sir."

"Mrs. Fisher?" Ashley had turned around and noticed Mary wasn't right behind them.

Mary couldn't stick around without it looking obvious that she was eavesdropping, so she continued out of the bank.

Steve was missing. Where could he be? And could he really have robbed his own bank?

THREE

When Mary, Rebecca, and Ashley arrived back at the bookstore, the only thing they could talk about was the robbery. They went over and over the events together but couldn't come up with any explanation for why Steve would do that.

"I know what happened was awful, but after all the work the shop owners put unto their prep for today, I hope this doesn't ruin all of Living History Day," Rebecca said. "I hope for their sakes the day goes on somewhat as planned."

"I hope so too," Mary said.

Henry entered the bookstore. "Are you ladies all right?" He looked worried. "I just heard about the robbery. Were you all at the reenactment?"

"Yes, and we're fine," Mary said, touched by his concern for them.

"It was kind of exciting," Ashley added, "after I got over being scared."

Rebecca and Mary glanced at each other and suppressed smiles.

Henry asked what happened, and they both recounted what they'd seen. Henry shook his head. "I just can't believe it of Steve."

"None of us can," Mary said.

"I'd better go. I'm supposed to be manning the information booth, but I nipped out to see how you all were."

"Thanks, Henry, but we don't want you to get in trouble."

"No chance of that." He winked at them and left.

As he left, Mary happened to see Sandra stagger out the front doors of the bank. She looked dazed, and her face was white as a sheet. Mary could guess that Sandra was overwhelmed by everything that just happened, maybe even a bit confused.

"She looks like she's going to faint," Mary said. "I'll bring her here for a cup of tea and a break from all that."

Mary hurried out of the store and approached Sandra. "Sandra? You okay?"

At the sound of Mary's voice, Sandra jumped as if she'd heard a gunshot. The poor young woman must be terribly upset about all this.

"Why don't you come to my store and sit down for a bit?" Mary gently took her by the elbow to guide her to the bookshop. "You look like you could use something hot to sip."

"T-thank you, Mary." The vulnerability in Sandra's face made her look younger than her twentysomething years.

Mary led Sandra to the reading area at the back of the store and sat her in one of the ivory twill armchairs, arranging a sea-green throw pillow at her back. "There, are you comfortable? How about some tea?"

Sandra nodded dumbly, and Mary bustled about, making a nice strong cup of tea with plenty of milk and sugar for the young woman. She placed the steaming mug in Sandra's hands and encouraged her to drink. After a little while, color seeped back into Sandra's cheeks.

Mary switched on the gas fireplace in the hearth and sat across from Sandra. "Feeling better?"

"Yes, thanks, Mary." Sandra closed her eyes, and a shudder ran through her. "It's just . . . every time I close my eyes, I see all the fake money strewn on the floor, the safe-deposit boxes blown open, Mr. Cooper tied up in the corner."

"Is Owen all right?" She remembered seeing the cuts on his face. "He wasn't hurt, was he?"

"Oh, he's fine. He has a few shallow cuts. Steve..." Sandra choked, then continued, "Steve used his gun—it was real, not fake—to blow open some of the safe-deposit boxes and take the contents, and Mr. Cooper was hit with some flying shrapnel, but he's all right. He was more shocked than anything else."

"That's what was in the bag he took from the bank? I thought that was full of fake money."

"No, we had put bags of fake money in the vault ahead of time, but he emptied the fake money onto the floor and looted the safe-deposit boxes instead."

"How many boxes were robbed?"

"It's confidential, so I'm afraid I can't tell you which boxes or how much was stolen."

Of course. Mary admired Sandra's discretion and didn't want to pry. "How horrible for the bank."

Sandra nodded miserably. Then tears began to flow quietly down her face.

"And you too." Mary stood up and went to Sandra, putting her arm around her and holding her as she cried.

They sat in silence for a while. Finally, Sandra said, "I can't believe Steve would do this."

"I have a hard time believing it too," Mary said. "Maybe they'll find Steve, and it'll all be a misunderstanding."

Sandra turned despairing eyes to her. "I want that to be true, but I just don't know."

Mary shook her head. "I think there's something wrong with all this. There was something wrong about the entire robbery...."

Sandra looked at Mary with curious eyes. "Like what?"

"I can't put my finger on it right now, but maybe later, when I've had a chance to think on it, it'll come to me."

They sat in silence until Sandra finished her tea. She set it on the small end table near her chair and rose to her feet. "Thank you for everything, Mary. I think I just want to go home now."

Mary walked with Sandra across the street to the bank parking lot and her car. She watched as Sandra drove off and then headed back to her store.

On the way, she saw her sister Betty hurrying down the sidewalk toward her with an anxious expression on her face.

"Bets, what's wrong?"

"A police officer said that Chief McArthur wants to speak to me." Betty wrung her hands together.

"But why? You weren't at the reenactment, were you?"

"No, I was helping Dora get ready for the fashion show at her dress shop. But one of the policemen talked to Eleanor, since she helped plan all this, and she mentioned I had been the one to talk to Steve about doing the robbery reenactment."

"There's nothing to be worried about."

"I know, but I feel almost like an accomplice. I gave him the chance to do this."

"Don't be silly." Mary put her hands on her sister's shoulders. "The chief just wants to know what Steve might have said to you. I'll come with you, if you'd like."

"I think I'd feel better if you did."

They crossed the street back to the bank. Betty told the officer guarding the front door that she'd been told Chief McArthur wanted to see her, so he let them inside.

At the lead banker's desk, Owen Cooper was sitting in the chair while a paramedic dabbed at some cuts on his face. Chief McArthur leaned against the desk, asking questions and nodding thoughtfully at Owen's answers, then taking notes in his notebook.

Betty hung back, waiting for them to finish, but then Mary had an idea. "Come on," she whispered, and they wandered to stand in front of Sandra's counter. Chief McArthur's back was to them, but they could clearly hear Owen's answers.

"No, Steve told me he was going to use fake money, not real money," Owen said.

"But you used an actual bank vault for the reenactment?" Chief McArthur asked.

"I would never have allowed using the main vault, but the safe-deposit vault was the original historical bank vault from 1870, and Steve wanted to use it for the reenactment." Owen sighed. "I wasn't entirely sold on the idea at first, but Steve pointed out that all the boxes were locked, and besides... this is Ivy Bay." Owen shrugged helplessly, as if that were explanation enough.

Chief McArthur gave a long, slow sigh.

"And the safe-deposit vault was going to be open for only about thirty minutes for the reenactment," Owen continued. "It seemed safe enough. I would never have thought...Steve, of all people..." Owen's voice sounded incredulous.

"Did Steve have any conflicts with anyone? Co-workers? Customers?"

At Chief McArthur's question, Mary suddenly remembered the snippet of the argument she'd overheard between Steve and Jerry Avakian at the back of the bank. Should she mention that? She chewed on her lip. With Steve and the valuables from the safe-deposit boxes missing, maybe she ought to tell the police so that they could pursue all leads. But she didn't want to think Jerry would have had anything to do with the robbery or Steve disappearing.

She didn't want to think Steve had anything to do with any of this either. She had chatted with him often enough when she went to the bank, and he just didn't seem the type of person to do something so awful. He seemed to genuinely love his work at the bank. And if he were going to steal money from the bank, why would he do it now, and in such a public way?

"Thank you, Mr. Cooper," Chief McArthur said to Owen, then turned toward Mary and Betty with a look that seemed to chide them for eavesdropping. "Would you ladies like to come here and sit down?"

"I would." Betty headed toward a chair with stiff movements. "I've been on my feet all morning."

And suddenly, Mary realized what she'd thought was wrong about the robbery reenactment. Steve had a slight limp because of an old motorcycle accident, but during the reenactment, the robber had swaggered into the bank. At the time, Mary had thought Steve was doing a good job getting into character and hiding his limp, but what if the robber hadn't been Steve at all?

Also, the robber hadn't spoken much during the reenactment, but when Mary had lent the historical book about the robbery to Steve, he had been excited about the opportunity to ham it up. Wouldn't he have done more than grunt two sentences?

And when she'd first heard the robber speak, Mary had been amazed at how differently he'd sounded from Steve's normal voice. She'd thought Steve was a good actor, but maybe it hadn't been that at all.

Betty was speaking to Chief McArthur about when Steve first talked to her about doing the reenactment. "He seemed excited about the idea. I thought it was because he'd been in drama in high school and he belongs to the local community theater group."

"How did he come up with the idea?"

"Mary gave him that book."

Chief McArthur's gray eyebrows rose as he looked at Mary.

She felt her neck warm. "I found a historical book about Elias Cowper, which mentions how he robbed Ivy Bay Bank in 1870. I lent it to Steve, which gave him the idea to do the robbery reenactment."

Chief McArthur scribbled in his notebook, and Mary's heart sank. This only made Steve look more and more guilty. But what else could she expect? The crowd of witnesses at the robbery and the fact he was now missing pointed to him taking the valuables from the safe-deposit boxes.

But did Mary really think the robber *wasn't* Steve? She didn't have any proof aside from a gut instinct that the robber's movements and voice didn't match Steve's.

"Chief McArthur, you know Steve," Mary pleaded. "You know he wouldn't do something like this."

The chief sighed heavily. "I don't want to believe any of our Ivy Bay residents could do something like this, but the facts are glaringly obvious: Steve arranged for the reenactment to happen and for himself to dress up as the robber, both Steve and the money are missing, and the rumors about the bank closing would give him a motive to steal from it and take off."

"But I don't think Steve was the robber," Mary said.

Chief McArthur looked at her with an intent expression. Betty said, "What do you mean, Mary?"

"I was watching the reenactment, and there was something about the robber that bothered me. I thought at first that Steve was being an exceptionally good actor, because he completely disguised his voice—the robber's voice didn't sound like Steve's at all. And then he lost his limp entirely when he was walking around the bank. I don't know how easy that is for someone who's been injured in a motorcycle accident, do you?" Mary gave Chief McArthur a pointed look.

"Do you have any proof it wasn't Steve?" Chief McArthur asked hopefully. "The other witnesses at the reenactment said it was him."

Mary shook her head slowly. "Not really. He was masked the whole time."

The chief sighed heavily again. "I wish there was more to go on. But I have to follow the evidence."

Mary understood his position, but everything inside her rebelled at the thought that Steve did this. It just didn't seem like him. And what was worse, if it wasn't Steve who did this, then where was he? Was he all right? *Lord,* she prayed, *if Steve didn't do this, I pray he's all right. And if he did...* She sighed. *I pray the police will find him soon.*

Mary hesitated, then said, "There is something I probably should tell you. About half an hour before the reenactment, the Courts' dog Pipp escaped. I was helping them look for him, and I saw him disappearing behind the bank. When I followed, I interrupted Jerry Avakian arguing with Steve." Mary added, "I don't want to get Jerry in trouble...."

"I understand."

"Jerry was towering over Steve and looked very threatening. Steve looked a bit nervous."

"What did they say?"

"I heard only a snippet of a sentence from Jerry. He said something like, 'If you weren't being so stubborn about the money,' and then he cut off when he saw me and Pipp."

"You're sure that's what you heard?" Chief McArthur was scribbling notes in his notebook.

"Yes, positive."

"And this happened behind the bank? Did you see anything else there?"

Mary blinked. "Like what?"

"Steve was supposed to change into the robber's costume behind the bank and then rush around to the front door to enter and 'rob' it. Did you see the costume lying around? Or anything else? The gun he used?"

"No, I'm afraid not. I was so uncomfortable at interrupting them that I grabbed the dog, apologized, and left as soon as I could. Oh," she said as she remembered, "when I apologized, Steve said that he and Jerry were done talking because he had to change for the reenactment."

"And then where did they go?"

"I don't know. I returned Pipp to the Courts and didn't see if Jerry and Steve left."

Chief McArthur said, "I'll be sure to speak to Jerry."

"I don't want to accuse him of anything...."

"I know, Mary. Don't worry."

His tone was businesslike, but the words were kind. She knew he'd handle this in a sensitive way because she'd seen it time and time again. He was a steadfastly dutiful police chief.

"Anything else you want to tell me?" he asked.

Mary and Betty shook their heads.

"Then if you'll excuse me..."

Mary and Betty headed out of the bank. "I feel so terrible about Steve," Betty said. "I've known him for years. This seems incredible."

"That's what makes me think he couldn't have done this," Mary said.

"But the police have good reason to suspect him."

"Hello, ladies." Johanna Montgomery appeared in front of them. She was still dressed in her Victorian outfit, and her face was slightly flushed. She was obviously here in her capacity as head reporter for the *Ivy Bay Bugle* because she had her notebook and tape recorder in her hands. "Were you at the reenactment?"

"I was," Mary admitted, "but I don't know what I can tell you that'd be different from what other people said." She was loath to tell Johanna about her suspicions about the robber not being Steve, at least until she'd had a chance to think about it more and perhaps do a little sleuthing of her own. To deflect any questions Johanna might ask, Mary said, "Are you here to speak to Chief McArthur? I think he's still inside."

Johanna nodded and headed toward the building.

"I'd better go," Betty said. "I'm scheduled to help with the moccasin demonstration at Cape Cod Togs."

"I'll see you at home later," Mary said.

Betty turned toward the upscale clothing store, but as Mary was about to cross the street back to her bookstore, her eyes fell on the small alley between the bank and the frame shop. Impulsively, Mary headed toward the alley. She'd left the alley quickly because of the argument, but now that she knew that Steve changed for the reenactment behind the bank, she wanted to take another look around. The police had probably already looked back here, but she kept thinking that if she'd been more observant at the time, she might have seen something.

She turned the corner to the back of the bank, which looked the same as when Mary had accidentally interrupted Jerry arguing with Steve. What had they been talking about? What money had Jerry been referring to? Did it have something to do with the robbery?

Mary walked through the small space. The back door of the bank stood firmly locked on one side, and on the other side was the back fence of the Chadwick Inn, which faced Water Street. A few scraggly bushes punctuated the narrow strip of land between the two properties, and the bank building on one side blocked out some of the sunlight.

The ground, which was packed dirt and gravel, looked like it had been trod by numerous people, possibly the police who had searched back here. Mary scanned the ground, the bushes, the edges near the walls.

She almost missed the long fibers, but her foot nudged some of them, making them jump on the ground. She peered closer.

They were long flax fibers, the exact same fibers she'd seen Jayne using in her spinning demonstration earlier today. These fibers had been specially prepared for spinning, meaning they hadn't simply fallen out of the plant they came from. They were long and very distinctive.

They were, without question, from Jayne Tucker's demonstration.

FOUR

Mary picked up the fibers. What were they doing here? She couldn't think why Jayne would have been back here. Mary looked more closely at the fibers and realized that they were twisted and a little crumpled. It looked like these fibers had been spun in that rope Jayne was making, but then were pulled out somehow.

But what connection would Jayne have to the robbery?

Mary then remembered seeing Jayne leave the robbery reenactment quite abruptly right in the middle of it, even before Sandra had announced that it had been a real robbery. At the time, Mary had thought it was the loud noise from the gun, but what if there was some other reason?

Also, Jayne's funds were still missing from the bank. Rumor had it that it was a substantial amount. What if Jayne held a grudge against Steve for not yet finding the money? Or maybe she thought the bank stole her money and she wanted some of it back? The missing funds would give Jayne a motive for being somehow involved in the bank robbery.

No, that was absolutely crazy. She could no more believe Jayne would do something like that than she could believe Steve would rob the bank. There had to be a simple explanation for why the rope fibers were back here. Maybe she gave the rope to someone.

She considered telling the police, but then reasoned that they wouldn't have overlooked these fine white fibers on the ground. They probably collected a few samples and left the rest, or maybe they didn't think it was worthwhile to investigate further into the fibers.

She searched for another few minutes but didn't find anything besides some nondescript cigarette butts and an empty soda can. She headed back down the alley toward the street.

As she approached, she heard a low roar that sounded like a crowd of people. Mary hurried out of the alleyway.

Several people were collected in front of the bank, and they all seemed to be trying to talk to—or rather, yell at—Owen Cooper. Chief McArthur stood in front of him, keeping the crowd at bay. Everyone was speaking in loud, strident tones, and Mary couldn't figure out what they were saying.

Johanna Montgomery stood at the edge of the crowd, scribbling in her notebook. Mary went up to her. "What happened?"

"Chief McArthur made an official statement that Steve Althorpe is their prime suspect for the robbery," Johanna replied. "He didn't seem very happy about it, and who can blame him? The thought of Steve robbing the bank is unbelievable."

"But why is everyone upset at Owen?"

Johanna's mouth tightened as she pointed out a young woman with a long, pinched face and rather unbelievably yellow hair. "Judith Dougher started it. She announced in front of everybody that because the police suspected Steve of robbing his own bank in broad daylight, and with the rumors about the bank being closed soon anyway, she was pulling her account from the bank. Then she started accusing Owen of running a shady business."

"That's terrible! Besides, Steve is only a suspect. He hasn't been accused of doing it."

Johanna gestured to the crowd. "It doesn't matter to them. Judith has been telling everyone to pull their accounts from the bank too."

"Poor Owen," Mary said. "This might ruin the bank. Even if the Neels Banking Group weren't planning on closing Ivy Bay Bank & Trust, they will after this."

"They might do that just because of the robbery," Johanna said.

Mary then saw Jayne hurrying out of her antique store and heading toward them, while looking in bewilderment at the crowd. As she approached Mary and Johanna, she asked, "What's going on?"

But at that moment, Judith Dougher spotted Jayne and made a beeline toward her. She spoke in a voice raised to carry across the crowd rather than a normal conversational voice. "You should be the first one to do this, Jayne."

Jayne looked like a deer caught in a car's headlights. "What are you talking about?"

"I'm pulling my account from the bank after everything that's happened today. And I'm doing it partly because of your missing funds too. Everyone knows how the bank still hasn't found your missing deposit. It's disgraceful."

"What?" Jayne's panicked eyes flew from Judith to the sight of Owen Cooper at the front of the bank. "Because of me?"

"Of course," Judith said in a ringing voice, but Mary stepped in front of her.

"Of course not, Jayne," Mary said firmly, trying to shield her from Judith's overbearing presence.

At that moment, Deputy Wadell came hurrying up. Perhaps Chief McArthur had radioed for him as soon as the crowd gathered, because he seemed to understand immediately what was going on. "Here, now, Judith, please leave Jayne alone." He bodily inserted himself between Judith and Jayne, and Judith grudgingly returned to the crowd that was still trying to harass Owen Cooper.

Supported by his deputy, Chief McArthur now raised his voice. "Everyone, calm down. There's a more appropriate place to speak to Mr. Cooper, and it's not on the steps of the bank. Go home and make an appointment with him tomorrow. And that means you too, Judith. I don't care if your husband is a lawyer. He still needs to abide by the rules, and you're not allowed to obstruct a place of business or accost Mr. Cooper."

Mary put her arm around Jayne. "Don't let her get to you, Jayne." Mary knew that Judith's husband, Marc, represented Daniel Hopkins in his case against the Emersons for the gristmill. Marc seemed reasonable, but who would have known his wife would be so belligerent?

"But I feel somehow responsible for what's happening." Jayne's worried gaze turned to the front of the bank, but the crowd was beginning to disperse. However, Mary would guess that several of them would be making appointments with Owen tomorrow to pull their accounts.

"You're not responsible at all," Mary said.

"Listen to Mary, Jayne," Johanna said. Mary had forgotten she was there.

Jayne nodded and made an effort to calm herself down. "You're right. I'm being a bit irrational. I'm just shocked at the entire robbery."

Mary remembered the flax fibers behind the bank, but Jayne was so upset right now Mary decided not to mention it just yet. However, she also remembered seeing Jayne leave the robbery early, and that seemed like a safe enough topic. "Were you in the bank for the reenactment?" Mary asked in a light voice.

Mary was surprised to see Jayne go white, then red. "Oh. Er, no."

Why would Jayne say that? Perhaps she figured that since she didn't stay for the entire reenactment, she didn't consider herself to have been there. Still, her reaction puzzled Mary.

"I should get back to the shop," Jayne said quickly, pulling away from Mary's supporting arm. Without bidding them good-bye, she abruptly turned and headed back to Gems and Antiques.

Mary blinked in surprise. Poor Jayne. She must be very upset.

"I'll see you later," Johanna said. "I have to get back to prep for my demonstration at the newspaper offices. Living History Day seems anticlimactic after the robbery, doesn't it?" She headed down the street.

Mary headed back to the bookstore in time to relieve Rebecca so she and Ashley could head to the newspaper offices. There weren't any customers at the moment, so she was left with her own thoughts.

She replayed in her mind over and over what she remembered of the robber when he'd walked around in the bank. She couldn't believe Steve would actually steal from the bank, even though the police obviously thought Steve was guilty of the robbery.

What if she was wrong? What if Steve really was guilty?

Well, there was only one way to find out. Mary didn't have much besides an understanding of Steve's character and a gut feeling about what she'd seen of the robber in the bank. Chief McArthur said he would be following the evidence, but Mary would follow the clues.

If she didn't think Steve robbed the bank, then that meant she needed to find out who did.

———

As Mary was arriving back at home that night, she happened to see her neighbor Sherry Walinski was also just arriving home from her job as secretary at Ivy Bay High School. Mary waved hello and walked over to Sherry, who was getting out of her car.

"Hi, Sherry." Mary then noticed that Sherry was wearing sweatpants and a sweatshirt under her coat and raised her eyebrows in surprise.

Sherry noticed her expression and laughed. "The school's off this week for fall break, so I don't have to dress for work. The principal came in wearing his jogging suit, and the vice principal was in holey jeans."

Mary grinned. "So it's the school's version of 'casual Fridays,' huh?"

"Exactly." Sherry grabbed her bag from the car and closed the door. "Come on in for some tea?"

"I'd love to."

Sherry opened the front door, and Mary wandered into Sherry's living room.

Sherry gestured to the dark-green corduroy couch. "Have a seat. I'll get the tea."

Mary settled down and glanced around the living room, which definitely showed signs that two teenage boys lived there. There was a game console hooked up to the large-screen television and a football hiding under the battered oak coffee table. Someone had also taken apart some electronic music player, and the pieces were on the coffee table in the midst of screwdrivers and a small soldering iron. However, the usual sounds of Sherry's sons were missing.

When Sherry returned to the living room with a tea tray, she said, "I just got this fantastic mint tea. The mint leaves are from a special farm in Canada."

"Sounds delicious. I love mint." As Sherry poured the tea, Mary guessed, "The boys are with their father tonight?"

"Yep. They'll be back at the end of the week." She handed Mary a cup of steaming tea.

Mary sipped. "This is wonderful. I think Betty would especially like this."

"They just started carrying this at Meeting House Grocers." Sherry served herself a cup. "It's nice to enjoy it with someone who appreciates it. The boys won't touch it." She made a face.

Mary laughed. "Well, they are teenage boys." Mary glanced around at the empty living room. "It must be quiet for you this week."

"I'm rather happy about that. Tyler's struggling with his English class, so he tends to procrastinate rather than do his homework, and I'm getting tired of nagging him to get it done. And Nate's been busy with football practice *and* class council. I don't have the heart to tell him to drop one of them."

"That would be a tough decision. They're both good for him to be involved in."

Sherry tipped her head to the side as she thought about it. "To be honest, I think I'd like him to drop class council."

"Really? Why?"

"I know the kids in class council, and I've been privy to information about what some of them have been up to." Sherry's eyes clouded with concern. "I don't really think those particular kids are the best influence for Nate."

"It must be quiet at the high school this week, because of fall break."

"Thank goodness for that." Sherry's eyes were wide. "Could you imagine what the kids would be like with the bank robbery? They'd be talking about it and not paying attention to any of the teachers." Sherry shook her head. "I can't believe it of Steve."

"Me neither. There must be some other explanation."

"And there're the rumors about the bank closing. Did you hear about that?"

"Yes. It would be awful if that happened."

"The timing of this whole robbery thing is horrible. Poor Owen and Sandra. I went over to Owen's house just to see how he was doing, but he was working late at the bank so I didn't see him."

"Sandra was so distraught that I gave her some tea at my shop to help her calm down."

"I hope she's all right?" Sherry asked.

"About as well as could be expected."

"I wish there was more we could do to make sure the bank doesn't close."

"I think if we support Sandra and Owen, they'll appreciate it."

Sherry nodded. "I think you're right. I'll see if I can visit her tomorrow. Gosh, the last time I sat and chatted with her was a month ago, after the volleyball tournament she won."

"She plays volleyball?"

"She coaches a club team."

Mary took a sip of tea. "A club team? She doesn't coach the school girls' volleyball team?"

"No, although the school did ask her a couple of times. Because of her job at the bank, she can only coach the club team, since they practice after her work hours."

"Oh, of course. How's her team doing?"

"At first, the club team didn't win a lot—they compete with other club teams in the state—but the girls had such improved self-esteem because of her that no one seemed to mind that they didn't have a great record. But the girls got better, and now they're competitive with the other teams in the league."

"That's wonderful. I didn't know that at all." This was an entirely new side to Sandra that Mary hadn't seen in her interactions with the young woman.

"Many of the parents in Ivy Bay love Sandra. They say she's very encouraging to the girls. And every year, she takes the team to Boston to volunteer for a week at a youth community center she used to go to when she was younger."

"That's wonderful. The girls must have a lot of fun."

"According to their parents, they love it. They get to go to a big city like Boston—with only Sandra supervising them." Sherry grinned. "And they meet new people at the community center."

"Didn't Tyler go to Boston for that swim meet? How did he do?"

She and Sherry chatted about her kids for a few more minutes before Mary took her leave.

That night, the robbery was all that Mary and Betty could talk about over their simple dinner of soup and sandwiches.

"Do you think Jerry Avakian had anything to do with it?" Betty said. "You seeing him arguing with Steve only minutes before the robbery seems strange, especially now that Steve's missing."

"It could have had nothing to do with the robbery."

"But he was talking about money."

"Steve does work at a bank."

Betty gave her a chagrined look. "Well, that's true. But the timing of the argument was a strange coincidence."

"It does seem that way, doesn't it? Almost as if he and Steve were partners. Or they could have not been partners at all, and Jerry's threatening words somehow caused Steve to disappear." Mary crumpled up her paper napkin. "I feel guilty for thinking of Jerry being involved at all. He's good friends with Henry, and Henry says he's a good man."

"But let's face it—everyone involved in this is someone we know." Betty yawned. "It's time for bed for me. I'm exhausted after helping out with Living History Day today."

"You go to bed, and I'll do the dishes."

"Are you sure?" But Betty looked longingly toward her bedroom.

Mary rose to her feet. "Absolutely. Good night."

"Good night."

Mary took their dinner plates to the sink and washed them absently, her mind still whirling around what had happened today—Steve and the robber, Jerry and Steve, those fibers behind the bank.

The fibers were definitely Jayne's. But who in the world would suspect Jayne of anything? And yet why were those fibers there? Jayne's answer about being in the reenactment seemed strange, especially after she'd left early. Mary wondered why she said she hadn't been there. Maybe she hadn't considered herself to have really been there, since she left early. But then, why hadn't she said that? It would have been more accurate. Mary couldn't help but feel like Jayne had intentionally lied.

Then again, Jayne had been upset at the time, with Judith Dougher saying she was pulling her account from the bank because of Jayne's missing money.

And really, why was Mary so hung up over this? So Jayne's fibers were found behind the back, so what? The police said that all evidence pointed to Steve robbing the bank.

Yet Mary couldn't get rid of her gut instinct that said the robber hadn't been Steve. And if that were the case, her mind was working through other, less obvious things that might point to a different explanation for what had happened.

So what could it be?

FIVE

The next morning, Mary woke up extra early. She hadn't slept well because she kept thinking about the robbery, and she realized she needed to write everything down.

She sat up in bed, got out a notebook and a pen, and began listing what she knew.

Robber:

Used real gun, not fake one. Mary hadn't known Steve even owned a gun, much less fired one. And, a fearful thought came to Mary: If a real gun *had* been involved, was Steve okay now? Where was he? And had he been hurt? Mary sent up a prayer for Steve, asking for safety, no matter what his role was in the robbery. He wasn't married and lived alone, although he seemed to have plenty of friends in Ivy Bay and an active social life. Surely one of his close friends would be thinking the same as Mary—that Steve couldn't have been the robber. But what could any of them do about it when Steve was missing?

Mary went on with her list.

Face and head covered. So it had been impossible to see if it was Steve or not.

Seemed to swagger or strut into the bank—no limp, or at least very well hidden. Would Steve have been able to hide his limp so well? Maybe, if it was only for a short time?

Voice seemed gruffer than Steve's. Did Steve disguise his voice, or was it someone else entirely?

Tied up Owen Cooper while they were in the safe-deposit vault. With what? Had Owen been perhaps tied up with the linen cord that Jayne had spun in her demonstration? Was that why there were fibers on the ground behind the bank? Had Steve had the linen cord with his robber costume and that's why the fibers came loose? Or was there another reason for the fibers being behind the bank?

Mary thought about the argument with Jerry. Would Jerry have used the rope to tie up Steve? Was that why he was missing?

All of this was speculation, but Mary wrote all these ideas down in her notebook so she could organize her thoughts better. She then continued with what she knew about the robber.

Used gun to shoot safe-deposit boxes and steal contents. Which boxes, and what did he steal? Was perhaps what the robber stole significant beyond financial reasons? Sandra hadn't been able to tell her because it was confidential, so Mary wasn't sure that she'd be able to find this out.

She then wrote down what she knew about Steve.

Steve Althorpe:

Lead Banker of Ivy Bay Bank & Trust for many years.

Helpful, friendly, walks with a limp from an old motorcycle accident.

Sandra said he loves working at the bank. Seemed happy with his job.

Rumors that Neels Banking Group will close the bank because it has closed other banks due to cost-cutting efforts. Was this motive for Steve to rob the bank and leave?

According to Todd at the Beacon Inn, Neels Banking Group reserved a room for someone to arrive today. An accountant or someone to review the bank's situation and determine if it should close? Or some other reason? Had Steve known who was coming and why? Did that have something to do with the robbery?

Steve's car gone from the parking lot. I remember seeing it yesterday morning, so he (or the robber) must have taken it.

Steve's boat is gone. The coast guard is searching for it. Did he leave town in the boat?

Steve wasn't at his house; police searched it. She wasn't sure if she would be able to get in, but she definitely wanted to go to his house to look around.

Mary couldn't think about anything else to do with Steve, so she wrote down what she remembered about Jerry.

Jerry Avakian:

Friend of Henry's. Owner of print and copy shop. I interrupted argument between Jerry and Steve behind the bank about thirty minutes before the reenactment. Jerry seemed belligerent and aggressive. Steve seemed nervous or awkward. Had he been intimidated by Jerry?

Jerry was saying angrily, "If you weren't being so stubborn about the money ... " What did he mean? What money? Did it have to do with the bank's money or something else? Why was Jerry so angry?

Why had they met behind the bank? Was Steve there preparing for the reenactment and Jerry followed him, or did they go back there deliberately for some privacy?

What happened after Mary left? Did Jerry leave? Did he do something to Steve? Did Steve do something else behind the bank besides prepare for the reenactment?

Mary also listed in her notebook: *Flax fibers behind the bank from Jayne's demonstration. Looked like they were pulled from spun cord, not smooth, unspun fibers.*

Why had there been flax fibers behind the bank? How had they gotten there? Had Jayne given her linen cord to someone? Jerry? Steve? Or was Jayne behind the bank for some reason? But why? Mary needed to ask her what she did with the cord after she spun it at the demonstration, without raising any flags that she vaguely suspected Jayne of involvement. Because she didn't. Jayne was a dear friend and a truly good citizen. There had to be a rational explanation.

As Mary reviewed her notes, the thought about the fibers behind the bank sparked an idea. The flax fibers could have been left behind the bank by several different people, of course, each with a different reason. Similarly, she'd been toying with an antique book planted at the crime scene in the mystery novel she was writing, but now she saw a multitude of possibilities as to why it was there—it was given to a reporter, who was at the crime scene for mysterious reasons of his own, or it was found by an heiress, who was at the crime scene because she was lured there, or it was a precious object owned by the captain.

With thoughts of her work-in-progress swirling along with thoughts of the robbery, Mary decided to give herself a break from the robbery and spend some time with her manuscript. She pulled up her laptop and opened the file with her novel. She skimmed what she'd written before to refresh herself, then started writing.

Before she knew it, it was two hours later and she'd gotten several pages written. She hadn't felt so inspired in a long time. But eventually, she heard Betty moving around downstairs and reluctantly knew she needed to get ready for work.

She read with satisfaction what she'd written and felt it was solid. She also made notes on how she wanted the mystery threads to progress so she had an idea of how the plot would unfold from this point on.

She saved her file and shut down her computer. She'd worked hard and felt like she was making good progress on her book, and it really had been a nice distraction from the constant stream of thoughts about the robbery that had been floating through her brain since yesterday. She went downstairs with more ideas for the story percolating in her head.

"Good morning," she said to Betty, and went to pour herself some coffee.

"Good morning. You look wide awake."

"I am, in fact. I've been up a couple of hours. I woke up early and got inspired to work on my novel."

"That's great." Betty's eyes shone. "What did you write? Did you kill someone off?"

Mary laughed. "You're incorrigible. No, nothing like that. But I wrote in three possible suspects all because of a book left at the crime scene."

"Who did you cast suspicion on?"

"The reporter, the heiress, and the captain."

Betty tapped her finger to her chin. "I bet it's the heiress. She has the most to lose."

"But then why would she risk losing it all in the first place?" Mary pointed out.

"Because she's in love?" Betty said.

Mary thought that might be too cliché, but then she had an idea: What if the heiress was in love, but not with a person anyone would suspect?

"Bets, you're brilliant." Mary jumped to her feet. "I've got to write this down."

She went upstairs and grabbed her laptop, bringing it downstairs with her. Betty told her, "Sit down. I'll make breakfast for you so you can write."

"Thanks, Bets." Mary pushed the button to turn on her computer. But after a brief moment, she realized there was something wrong. The screen was still black.

Alarm fluttered in her throat as she bent over the laptop. She couldn't hear the hard drive whirring as it always did, and there was nothing on the screen.

She manually restarted the computer by holding down the power button and stood in front of it, waiting.

The same thing happened—or rather, the same things didn't happen. The hard drive was silent, and the screen remained stubbornly blank.

Dread twisted in her stomach, making her feel queasy. This couldn't be happening! The laptop had been perfectly fine earlier this morning. Why wouldn't it start up?

Had she lost everything on the computer, including her manuscript?

The thought made her want to cry and wail. She had been so faithful about saving the file as she worked on it, and she distinctly remembered saving it just before she shut her computer off earlier this morning.

But an insidious voice asked her, *Did you back up your file?*

Mary slumped into a chair at the kitchen table. She had an online backup system where she could send her files as a secondary storage place for them, but she hadn't used it this morning. She'd been so triumphant about getting so much done, and yet she'd forgotten this crucial step! Having so much inspiration come so unexpectedly had made her completely overlook backing up her file.

"Here you are." Betty set some eggs in front of her, then saw Mary's face. "What's wrong?" Her voice rang with concern.

"I'm, uh...fine..."

"You are absolutely not fine. Your face is as white as the countertop." Betty sat next to Mary. "What happened?"

"I forgot to back up my file. And now, my laptop w-won't start." Mary was mortified as her voice broke, but she felt as if her insides were being mashed around in a stand mixer. All her work from earlier this morning, gone.

"Oh no." Betty laid a hand on Mary's arm and squeezed.

"I'm...I'm not sure what to do."

Betty straightened. "I'll tell you what. Let's look in the phone book for a computer-repair shop. There has to be some computer genius out there who can fix your computer at least enough for you to get your file back."

At Betty's words, Mary realized she already knew a computer genius. "I wonder if Bea's granddaughter Megan can help me."

"Bea Winslow?"

"Yes, her son's daughter Megan belongs to the computer club at school. I was just chatting with her yesterday."

"Why don't you give Bea a call? It's early, but I know she gets in to work by seven thirty."

Mary called with a bit of trepidation since it was rather early in the morning. She hoped Bea was already at work. Thankfully, Bea answered quickly with a cheerful, "Hello, county clerk's office. Bea speaking."

"Hi, Bea. This is Mary Fisher."

"Hi, Mary. What can I do for you?"

"Actually, would you be able to ask Megan for some help for me? My laptop worked fine earlier this morning, but now it won't turn on."

"Uh-oh. That happened to me once, so I know that sick feeling in your stomach you must have right now. Let me call Megan and see. I don't think she has anything planned for today—for this entire week, actually."

"Thanks, Bea."

Mary sat at the kitchen table and waited with barely held impatience for Bea to call her back. Finally, Betty told Mary to stop bouncing her leg because she was making the wooden floor squeak.

Mary gave her sister a chagrined look. "Sorry."

"Oh, I know you're worried."

Mary took a sip of her cooling coffee, trying to calm herself, when the phone rang. She leaped up to answer it. "Hello?"

"Hi, Mary. It's Bea. Megan said she'd love to help. You can stop by her house to drop off the laptop." Bea rattled off the address, which was just on the outskirts of downtown Ivy Bay, near the beach.

"Thanks, Bea." Mary got off the phone and grabbed up her laptop, but Betty halted her.

"Going in your pajamas?" she said drolly.

Mary looked down at her flannel pj's and laughed. "I guess not."

Megan's house was close enough that Mary could have walked, but she elected to drive to get there a little faster. She parked in front of the sweet little bungalow painted a soft sea-green with white trim and walked up the flagstone path to the front door.

The woman who answered the door, Megan's mom, Angela, looked exactly like Megan, with hazel eyes and fine, straight hair in the same shade of brown. Megan's mother wore hers tied back in a ponytail, and that with her welcoming smile made her look too young to have a teenage daughter. "Hi, Mary. Bea told us you were coming."

"Thank you so much for letting me stop by so early."

"Bea told us you had a computer emergency. We've had some of those, so we understand *completely*."

As Mary entered the cozy living room, furnished in sea greens and blues, Megan appeared from a hallway at the far end of the room. She wore a faded T-shirt with John Lennon's face on it, which made Mary smile.

"Hi, Mrs. Fisher." Megan seemed to stand taller today, with a confident, businesslike attitude that sat well on her young shoulders. "I'm sorry about your computer, but I hope I can fix it for you."

"Thank you so much for agreeing to do this." Mary handed her the laptop bag, which held her computer and power cable. "I hope it doesn't take too much time. I don't want to ruin your fall break with my silly computer problems."

Megan's eyes slid away from hers. "Oh, it's not a problem. I don't have anything else planned."

Megan set up the computer on the wooden coffee table, and Angela said, "Mary, would you like some coffee?"

"I had a cup at home, thanks. If I have any more, I'll be a nervous wreck."

Angela laughed. "I'll leave you to it, then." She headed down the hallway Megan had come from.

Megan was trying to turn the computer on, but now a frown line appeared between her eyes. *"Hmm."*

That didn't sound very promising. Mary sat on the couch next to her, her heart sinking. "I'm mostly interested in getting my manuscript file off the hard drive. I wrote quite a bit a few hours ago, but I forgot to back it up on my online backup service, and I don't want to lose it all."

"Well, I have good news and bad news," Megan said. "The good news is that there's a good chance that your hard drive is fine and your files are safe. However, I won't know for sure until I can figure out what's wrong."

Mary almost wanted to laugh at how mature Megan's computer expertise made her seem. But she was too impressed—and dismayed about her computer—for laughter, and she certainly didn't want to embarrass Megan. "What's the bad news?" Mary said.

Megan grimaced. "The bad news is that the reason your computer won't turn on might be a hardware issue. I'll have to figure out what's wrong, and that might take some time. It also might cost money if you have to replace components."

"How much?"

"Probably not as much as a new laptop. I'll let you know before I buy anything, of course. But first, I need to ask if this is still under its manufacturer's warranty?"

"No, it's not."

"Okay, good. I wouldn't want to open it up if it was still under warranty because that might void the warranty."

"Do you think you can fix it?" Mary clasped her hands tightly together.

Megan's answer was professional and polite. "I'll do my best."

Her answer didn't really make Mary feel very confident, but she supposed it was better for Megan to tell her the truth rather than getting Mary's hopes up.

"You don't have to stick around, Mrs. Fisher," Megan said. "You can go to work or something. I'll call you if I find anything."

Mary figured the teen probably wouldn't want her hovering while she worked, anyway. "Thanks for doing this for me, Megan. I really appreciate it, whether you can fix it or not. Here's my business card. I'll be at the bookstore all day."

Megan walked Mary to the door, and just before saying good-bye, she said, "I'll do everything I can."

Mary smiled. "I know you will."

She drove back home where Betty was washing up the breakfast dishes. "That was quick."

"Megan said she'd do her best and call me later. I need to go to the bookstore, anyway. If I'm doing something, maybe it'll take my mind off of it."

Mary packed Gus in his carrier and also grabbed the newspaper, since she hadn't had a chance to read it this morning, and headed toward her store. The morning was a bit crisp but still clear, a lovely fall day in Ivy Bay. She waved to a few farmers in the cranberry bog, who waved cheerfully back at her.

She opened up the shop and let Gus out, and he immediately went sniffing at all the corners, catching up on all the new smells in the store that he'd missed because Mary had left him home yesterday. He gave Mary a reproachful look as if to say, "How in the world did you manage yesterday without me?"

Rebecca arrived shortly after with Ashley, who was carrying a backpack stuffed full of books.

"Goodness, are those schoolbooks?" Mary asked the young girl.

Ashley giggled. "No, we went to the library yesterday, and I got a bunch of books to read this week, since there's no school."

Rebecca added, "If I hadn't taken her, she'd have been bouncing off the walls."

Ashley had set her backpack down and was sorting through them. "All of these are books you don't have yet, Mrs. Fisher. If I like them, I'll tell you so you can order them."

"That's great, Ashley." Mary had initially had doubts about hiring Rebecca because she'd had to bring Ashley to work with her sometimes, but now she couldn't imagine the store without both of them. Ashley, especially, had been so helpful with customers, children and adults, who came into the store, and her thoughtful recommendations for books Mary should order for the shop's children's section were always dead-on.

However, just when Mary could have really used a busy day, the store was a bit emptier than usual. Ashley lounged in the upholstered bathtub in the children's section, her legs dangling as she read a book. Rebecca sat behind the front counter and stared into space. "When does the next book shipment come in?"

"Not until Friday." Mary dusted the shelves, even though she'd done that just a couple of days ago. Meanwhile, her mind whirled around and around. Why hadn't she remembered to back up her manuscript file? What if Megan couldn't fix her computer or retrieve her file? She shouldn't be so pessimistic. Maybe Megan would be able to fix her computer, and Mary would at least be able to send her manuscript to her backup service. She should have backed up her file. Maybe she needed to prepare herself for the worst and expect to have lost the file. All that work, gone! She went back to the front counter and couldn't stop herself from heaving a sigh.

Rebecca gave her an odd look. "Is everything going okay?" she asked tentatively.

So much for keeping her problems to herself. Mary sighed. "It's nothing for you to worry about. My laptop died this morning, and I'm worried I lost my manuscript file."

"Oh no!" Rebecca's face reflected the horror that Mary was feeling. "That happened to me once. Are you having someone look at it?"

"Yes, Bea Winslow's granddaughter is a computer whiz, so she's taking a look today."

"If she can't fix it, I can recommend someone I used for my computer. He's about forty minutes away from Ivy Bay, but he's very good."

"Thanks," Mary said gratefully, although she did hope the problem was easy enough that Megan could fix it.

With nothing left to do around the shop, she opened up the newspaper and saw a photo of the robber from the bank. The caption underneath said that it had been taken by a spectator in the crowd using his cell phone. Mary supposed that the lower resolution of the cell phone was why the picture was a little blurry when printed in the newspaper.

Yes, she remembered seeing people in the bank with cell phones and cameras, and some had been taking videos of the reenactment. Would any of them have posted something on the Web? So many people these days liked posting photos and videos online. It was worth looking into.

She went to the store computer and searched for "Ivy Bay Bank & Trust robbery" and came up with multiple hits. Some were online newspaper articles, but there were several on a video Web site where people uploaded their own digital videos. Mary clicked on that.

There were three videos of the robbery that people had taken with their cell phones. One was by someone at the back of the crowd and didn't show the robber very well, although the person got a good shot of Sandra coming out to make her dramatic announcement. The second video was much better, and Mary watched with interest.

The camera jumped when the robber fired the gun, and the robber went out of the camera view for a moment, but then the videographer refocused on the robber. Mary watched the robber strut into the bank, and she knew in an instant that it wasn't Steve.

The man put weight easily on his left leg. Mary knew for a fact that Steve limped and couldn't fully put weight on his left leg. He'd had multiple surgeries and gone through a great deal of physical therapy even to be able to walk on it.

But the robber swaggered and put weight on his left leg, far more than Mary had ever seen Steve do. At one point, he even shifted his weight to his left side as he stood there, which Mary knew Steve would never do, even if he were in character, because it was too physically difficult.

She checked to make sure the video wasn't flipped to its mirror image. No, she could clearly read the message on a bank sign, so it was correct. The robber did not favor his left leg the way Steve did.

But was this proof enough for the police? It didn't matter if they couldn't find Steve.

If this robber wasn't Steve, then once again she wondered: Where was he? Was he all right? What had this man done to him?

Mary felt another wave of concern welling up inside her chest. She had to think clearly. She had to find Steve. She had to question anyone who seemed suspicious because they might know where Steve was.

She realized with a jolt that if this robber wasn't Steve, time was of the essence.

SIX

The next hour in the shop was rather boring because they had only a few customers, and they each entered the shop one at a time. Either Mary or Rebecca spoke to them to see if they needed any help, but all the customers that morning preferred to browse on their own.

Mary remembered what she'd overheard yesterday about Steve's home and his boat. Now that they had a free moment, she ought to check both of them out for herself.

She turned to Rebecca. "I just remembered a couple of errands I need to run, and since the shop isn't very busy right now—"

Rebecca waved her hand before Mary even finished her sentence. "Go ahead. I can hold down the fort."

Mary donned her coat and stepped out of the store, then turned right to head home to pick up her car. She knew Steve lived near the docks, which was perfect since she also wanted to ask about his boat. She knew the police had already done so, but she hoped to find something the police might have overlooked.

The salt-scented air seemed to clear out her mind and help her think. She took a deep breath. She was grateful every day that she came here to live with Betty. What a beautiful town Ivy Bay was.

As she walked, Mary looked across the street at Gems and Antiques. Jayne was standing on the sidewalk, a little ways down from her store, but not in view of the windows of the Black & White Diner. Jayne seemed to be talking earnestly to someone, and Mary peered closer to see who it was. The man had a seedy appearance, with nondescript clothes in grays and browns and a ferret-like face. Mary had a slimy feeling when she saw him and wondered why Jayne was talking to him. She'd never seen the man in town before.

Jayne's face was in one-quarter profile, but then she turned her face sideways and Mary got a good look at her expression. She looked distressed, which worried Mary. What was wrong? Did this have something to do with the fact that Jayne had seemed down and upset for the past week? Did this have to do with her leaving the reenactment in the middle of it and being so abrupt with Mary yesterday? Or did this have to do with her missing funds from the bank?

Mary chided herself. It could be any number of things, and she was only feeling suspicious of her friend because of the flax fibers she'd found behind the bank. She had forgotten to ask Jayne about that, but she didn't want to interrupt her when she was talking to this man. She'd find a way to talk to Jayne later this morning, maybe after she went to Steve's house and the docks.

She continued on, but before she got very far, someone else caught Mary's eye. A tall, thin man in a suit and expensive-looking wool coat walked down the opposite sidewalk toward the bank. He looked intelligent as well as smartly dressed.

He entered the bank, just as Mary suspected he would. Was he the person from the Neels Banking Group who was to have checked into the Beacon Inn today?

As Mary continued down the street, she wondered how the bank would fare in light of the robbery. She was afraid the Neels Banking Group would close Ivy Bay Bank & Trust because of that. It was terribly embarrassing.

She supposed they might take into account if Ivy Bay Bank & Trust was doing well financially, but no one outside of the bank employees knew if it was doing well or not. However, Mary would have thought that if it were doing well, they wouldn't send an accountant to Ivy Bay to look over the bank's records.

She realized she shouldn't speculate too much. She didn't know for certain if that was who that man was and why he was here.

At the corner of Ivy Lane and Main Street, she met up with Bob Hiller, the town mailman, who was chatting with one of Mary and Betty's neighbors, Cathy Danes. Mary loved the roses Cathy cultivated in her front yard.

Bob smiled and greeted her, and Cathy gave her normal slightly nervous smile.

"How are you doing?" Bob asked cheerfully, while adjusting his mailbag. Bob was in his sixties, with slightly hunched shoulders, and he'd been the town mailman for over forty years. "The bookstore isn't closed, is it? I have some mail I was going to deliver in a few minutes."

"No, I'm going on a few errands, and Rebecca is minding the shop." She smiled at Cathy. "You look like you're off on a walk."

"I'm just coming *back* from a walk," Cathy said. "The dunes were nice, but a little chilly for me." She had tucked her hair under a chunky woolen cap and had a matching scarf wound around her neck. "I was telling Bob that he needs a thicker jacket."

"I'd like a fancy wool coat like that gent we just saw walking down Main Street."

"I saw him enter the bank." Cathy wrung her hands together. "I hope the bank's going to be okay. I wouldn't want it to close."

"No one wants it to close," Bob said. "I've talked with lots of people, and everyone's worried." Bob was friendly with everyone, but he was also the town gossip. Mary had to admit that if he said the atmosphere among the residents was grim, he probably knew what he was talking about.

"Judith Dougher said we should pull our accounts from the bank before it goes under," Cathy said.

"I heard a few other people intend to do that today, but I don't know if you really want to listen to Mrs. Dougher," Bob said with a grimace. "Besides, if you pull your account, then the bank will definitely go under. Wouldn't you rather the bank stay open?"

"Will it stay open after the robbery yesterday?" Cathy's hand fluttered to her throat. "How awful for that to happen. I wonder what was stolen. And why safe-deposit boxes? Was Steve trying to steal something in particular?"

"I did chat with one person whose deposit box was opened," Bob said. "Obviously they didn't say what was taken, but apparently, the robber shot up the four largest boxes and took the contents of those. It doesn't look like Steve was looking for anything in particular." Bob shook his head. "I can't believe Steve Althorpe would rob his own bank. It just doesn't seem like him."

"But then where is he? And where are the things he took?" Cathy wrung her hands again. "It looks like he just took what he could and ran."

Mary sighed. It did seem that way, but she was of the same mind as Bob. She couldn't believe Steve would do that, and the video of the robber seemed to indicate that it wasn't him. If there was another explanation, she would do her best to find it.

When she finally arrived home, she surprised Betty, who was resting on the couch. Concerned about her rheumatoid arthritis, Mary asked, "Are you all right?"

"Oh, I'm fine," Betty said. "Just being a bit lazy this morning. I have to meet with Eleanor this afternoon to go over Living History Day reports and things."

Mary knew that her sister being on her feet all day yesterday probably took more out of her than she was admitting to. "Since I'm home, is there anything I can get for you?"

"Well, a cup of tea would be nice."

"I was just going to get one before I headed back out, so that's perfect."

Mary made the tea and found a couple of tea cookies, and she sat across from Betty as the two of them enjoyed a snack and a short chat.

"With everything that happened, I never got a chance to talk to you about Living History Day. How did it go for you? I know you and Eleanor put in a ton of work."

Betty chatted about the different demonstrations she'd helped with, some emergencies avoided, and some feedback she had received from a couple of parents of children who'd enjoyed the day.

They were interrupted by the telephone, and when Mary answered it, a chirpy voice said, "This is Missy Stanton from Ivy Bay High School. Could I please speak to Betty Emerson?"

"One moment please." Mary turned to Betty. "Missy Stanton from the high school?"

"Oh." Betty sat up straighter and held her hand out for the phone. "Missy thought Living History Day would be a good project for her students to help out with next year."

Mary gave her the phone, then went to put away the tea things and get her car keys. She waved good-bye to Betty, who was still sitting on the couch and talking animatedly with Missy, before she headed out the door.

She drove to Steve's house, a small bungalow near the docks. She parked in front, right next to a squad car. She wasn't surprised to see a police officer there at the house, since the bank had just been robbed yesterday. Perhaps there were more officers inside gathering evidence, or they were just temporarily safeguarding the house for some other official reason.

The police officer in the car got out when she did and approached her. "Hello, there, ma'am," he said in a friendly way, and for a moment, Mary thought he might let her waltz inside.

"Hi, there." She smiled. "I already told Chief McArthur this, but I lent Steve a historical book about the original bank robbery, and I wanted to see if I could find it. I think it might be in Steve's house, and it might have a clue as to the robbery that happened yesterday." It wasn't the only reason she was here, but she couldn't exactly add that she wanted to look around Steve's house for any clues as to his whereabouts. Since the police suspected Steve, Mary thought she had a good chance of finding a clue as to Steve's innocence or the truth as to what really happened at the bank.

The officer smiled and nodded.

Mary continued, "So would it be all right if I went inside to look around? I promise not to touch anything."

"Sorry, ma'am," the officer said, still smiling.

Now Mary knew the officer probably thought she was nuts. She took a different angle. "I'm sure the officers have been through everything inside," she said, trying to sound reasonable, "so it's not as if I can disturb anything. And I won't take more than a minute or two."

"Nope. Sorry, ma'am."

"How about if I look in through the windows from the outside? You can come with me to watch me."

"Nope. Sorry, ma'am."

Mary had to fight to not huff in impatience. The officer was only doing his duty, she supposed. "When do you think I could come back to look inside?" she asked.

"You'll have to speak to Chief McArthur about that."

Would he really let her do that? Well, no harm in asking. "I will. Thank you, Officer."

"No problem, ma'am." He gave that wide smile again and escorted her to her car.

She got inside, but then instead of driving off, she took out her cell phone and called the police station. She might as well ask the chief right now in case he might give her permission to look around. "Could I please speak to Chief McArthur?" she asked when her call was answered.

The dispatcher put her through, but Chief McArthur sounded a bit impatient when he answered, "McArthur."

"Hello, Chief. This is Mary Fisher. I wondered if you might give me permission to look inside Steve's house for that book I mentioned to you."

He sighed. "Mary, you know I can't do that."

"But I think the book might say what the robber did when he disappeared. As I remember, the original robber, Elias Cowper, was infamous for seeming to disappear into thin air after his robberies."

"Much as I could use any help on the case, Mary, I simply cannot break the rules and allow you inside the house of a suspected felon when that felon is still missing."

"Even if Steve may not have been the robber?" Mary persisted. "I saw some of the videos of the robbery, and the man doesn't look like Steve. Steve has a limp, and the man doesn't."

"I'm afraid that's not good enough evidence to clear Steve of suspicion."

She knew he was right. She stared in frustration at Steve's house, so close and yet so far. She hated to sound like a dog with a bone, but she also trusted her gut instinct that something was wrong here. "Do you know *when* it might be all right for me to look inside Steve's house?"

"Maybe after we have him in custody," the chief said, "and Steve himself gives you permission."

Mary knew what the chief was really saying: *Don't count on it.* So if the robber wasn't Steve, she needed to find something else to point to where he was and who the real robber was.

Mary had a sudden vision of herself, dressed in all black and sneaking into Steve's house in the dead of night. The picture made her want to giggle, which she tried to stifle with the officer still surveying her in her car. He probably thought she was crazy.

"Tell you what," Chief McArthur said, "I'll have one of the officers look inside the house for the book when we have time. All right?"

She supposed it was better than nothing. He could have completely refused to listen to her wild assertions about a historical robbery book. "Yes. Thank you, Chief," Mary said. "I'll let you get back to work." She said good-bye and disconnected the call.

She couldn't—legally—get into Steve's home right now, but there wasn't anything keeping her from walking the docks, was there? She wanted to see if she could look around where the boat had been berthed to search for clues. Also, she might be able to ask people about Steve's boat and when it had disappeared. There wasn't any harm in trying, and they might be more willing to speak to her than a police officer.

When Mary got to the docks, she parked and got out of the car. As she strolled down the weathered boards, she watched the occasional boat cruise by. Seagulls swooped lazily overhead, and the breeze from the bay blew gently on her face. A day like today, enjoying the surroundings, made her so grateful for all the Lord had given to her. The work she'd done on her manuscript that morning had been a gift from the Lord too. If she got it back, that would be wonderful, but if she didn't, she knew that God would help her to work on the manuscript again.

After a while, she strolled closer to the docks where the boats were berthed. She didn't know where Steve's boat was usually docked, so she asked a man who was cleaning his fishing boat.

He squinted and pointed down toward the middle section. "You can't miss it," he told her. "Lots of yellow tape and police."

Mary thanked him, but her heart sank. Like when she arrived at Steve's house, she had a feeling she wouldn't be allowed to poke around where Steve's boat had been berthed. She headed out toward the boats, and a cool autumn wind swirled around her, carrying the scent of brine. But because of the sunshine, the wind wasn't too chilly, and Mary walked comfortably in her jacket.

She wasn't the only one drawn to the docks because of Steve's boat. Several tourists gathered behind yellow Do Not Cross police tape strung on stands around an empty berth where she assumed Steve's boat had been. An officer was there and would warn someone if he or she stepped too close to the tape.

The berth itself was rather unimpressive, looking just like the neighboring berth except that it was empty. Below, the water slapped against barnacle-coated pillars. From where

Mary stood, she couldn't see any trash on the ground or personal items left behind, no footprints left on the ash-gray wooden boards. Rope coiled against a pillar, but other than that, it was empty of anything but yellow police tape.

That was rather anticlimactic. Mary turned away and headed back down the dock. She could try to speak to people about Steve's boat. She wondered if she'd find out anything more than what Deputy Wadell had told the police chief yesterday. Would one of the fishermen tell her something that they didn't tell the police?

On the section she was walking, there were some huge, expensive yachts and also some weather-beaten fishing boats. Some of the boats were closed up since the owners were out of town or enjoying somewhere warmer.

She had turned a corner on the wooden pier when, directly ahead of her, Jerry Avakian was about to get onto a sleek, expensive-looking boat. He was speaking to a man Mary didn't recognize, who had a deeply tanned face and sunglasses that glinted in the sun. The man wore a bright-blue nautical Windbreaker with a logo on the sleeve that signified it was from a pricey name brand.

For a man who had been arguing with Steve about money, Jerry seemed to be at home around the large boat. He still had one foot on the dock when he caught sight of Mary—she was hard to miss since she was walking toward them. Mary nodded and smiled at him. "Hello, Jerry. Nice day, isn't it? Going out on the water?"

At the sound of her voice, Jerry hesitated, as she had hoped he would. It enabled her to reach his side before he could escape her.

Because it certainly looked as if Jerry wanted to escape her. His smile to her was tight, and he glanced nervously at the stranger, who stood on the boat a few feet away. But Jerry couldn't simply nod to her and turn away or it would be rude, so he stopped and said, "Hi, Mary. Yes, we're about to head out."

The man, on the other hand, seemed relaxed, and Mary turned to him with a friendly smile. He responded with one of his own, flashing white, even teeth.

"Hello," Mary said to the stranger. "I'm Mary Fisher."

"I'm Gibson Overfield," the man said in a hearty voice.

Jerry still looked like he might be trying to gracefully get away from her, so Mary said to him, "I ought to apologize for cutting into your conversation yesterday with Steve. I was so embarrassed that I hurried away quickly."

A hint of red might have crept up Jerry's neck, but his olive complexion made it hard for Mary to be sure. "That's all right, Mary. No need to apologize. You were helping return that dog to its owners."

"Yes, the Courts got Pipp back safe and sound," she said gaily, her mind racing for ways to engage in conversation with Gibson Overfield.

However, Jerry was too quick for her. "Well, we'd better get going, Gibson. Good-bye, Mary. See you 'round." Jerry climbed into the large boat and turning his back toward Mary, began speaking to Gibson in a low, businesslike tone while leading him deeper into the boat.

Mary hesitated on the pier next to the boat, but then made a graceful exit. Jerry certainly hadn't wanted to talk to her. Or was it that he hadn't wanted her to speak to the stranger?

What had their meeting been about? It seemed important, at least to Jerry.

It made her even happier that she managed to get his attention before he got on that boat and forced her way into an introduction. She had wanted the man to give her his name so she could look it up later. She wasn't sure she'd find anything, but he looked relatively wealthy. He might own a business or something like that, so she figured she had a good chance.

Mary wondered why Jerry hadn't wanted to talk to her. Was it because he was embarrassed about her interrupting his argument with Steve? His behavior seemed a little suspicious after what she overheard yesterday. And what was he doing with such a nice boat? She didn't know he owned one.

Mary wondered if she should talk to Henry about Jerry, since they were friends, but she was loath to bring it up. She didn't have any type of proof, just suspicions based on the interrupted argument and now the awkwardness with Jerry and Gibson Overfield at that beautiful boat. If Mary mentioned those things, Henry might think she was accusing Jerry of something and get upset at her.

But maybe she *was* accusing Jerry of something. She'd seen him arguing heatedly with Steve, and then the person who robbed the bank hadn't been Steve. Did Jerry know something about where Steve was?

SEVEN

◆◆◆

Mary continued walking along the docks, enjoying the unseasonably warm sunshine. She looked for any fishermen around that she could talk to, but it looked like many of them were either still out with the tide or maybe had already returned from their early-morning fishing and sold off their catches. She stopped to chat with a couple of fishermen hanging around the docks, but they didn't know anything about Steve's boat.

Mary checked her watch and realized she should get back to the bookshop. When she returned to her store, Rebecca was ringing up a customer at the old-fashioned register while another customer browsed the new-releases table. With a quick smile to Rebecca, Mary approached the customer with a friendly, "Hello, how are you doing today? Is there anything I can help you with?"

Fifteen minutes later, the second customer had left with Lorna Barrett's latest cozy mystery tucked into a bag with its signature Mary's Mystery Bookshop sticker.

"Were things busy while I was gone?"

"Not too," Rebecca said. "There was one mom who came in with her two kids, and Ashley took care of them. She convinced their mother to buy each of them a book."

"Thanks, as always, Ashley," Mary called toward the children's nook, where Ashley was reading.

"No problem, Mrs. Fisher," Ashley said with a small giggle.

Another customer came in then, and they were busy until almost one. Mary turned to Rebecca. "Did you want to take your lunch break now?"

"Yes, Mom, I'm starving," Ashley said in a plaintive voice as she got up from the reading nook.

Rebecca snorted in laughter. "Yes, I can see you're perishing from hunger. Okay, let's go."

After they'd gone, since the store was empty of any customers, Mary went to the store computer and did an Internet search for Gibson Overfield, the man she saw with Jerry on the nice boat.

The search engine gave her more results than she expected, so she limited the search to Massachusetts. The very first entry was for Gibson Overfield, a boat broker. When she clicked on the Web site, she saw a photo of the exact same man she'd just met.

A boat broker. Was Jerry about to buy that nice boat? Was that the business they'd been talking about?

Or was Gibson Overfield one of Jerry's customers? Mary checked out more information about Mr. Overfield's business and discovered he was based in Boston. He couldn't be Jerry's customer—Mr. Overfield wouldn't be traveling that far just for a print and copy shop, and there were many such shops in Boston.

So the business Jerry was talking with Mr. Overfield had to be about boats. But if Jerry were buying a boat, how did he get the money? Had he been saving it?

Or—and the thought chilled her—did he indeed take Steve's place and rob the bank, and now he was using his new funds?

Could Jerry be buying the boat in order to get away? But if that were the case, wouldn't it have made more sense for him to have left immediately after the robbery rather than lingering in town?

Perhaps if he'd left too soon after the robbery, it would make him look suspicious, especially since all the evidence and Steve's disappearance made it look like Steve had robbed the bank, not Jerry.

And if Jerry had taken Steve's place, what would he have done with Steve? Where was he? Maybe Steve was working with Jerry?

She remembered Steve's missing boat. If Jerry did rob the bank, why not just take Steve's boat rather than buy a new one? Well, but the description would have been given to the coast guard right away, so it was safer not to have taken Steve's boat. Or perhaps Jerry was in partnership with Steve, and Steve had taken his boat and left, and Jerry was meant to follow and find him later?

Mary analyzed her thoughts and almost laughed out loud. All of this was pure speculation, and a bit far-fetched at that. Jerry taking Steve's place and robbing the bank...Jerry in partnership with Steve...Jerry planning to buy a boat to make his escape...How ludicrous it sounded, just in her own head.

Still...Mary looked at Gibson Overfield's Web site. Why had Jerry been talking to him?

She knew Gibson might still be out with Jerry and certainly wouldn't have returned to his office in Boston yet, but she picked up her cell phone and punched in the number on the Web site. Immediately, Gus jumped up onto the counter, purring and rubbing his head against her hand.

She idly stroked him while she listened to the ringing of the boat broker's phone. Then a woman's voice answered, "Hello, Gibson Overfield's office. How may I help you?"

Mary hesitated only a fraction of a second. She wasn't entirely sure what she was looking for. She supposed she could try to find out about the boat Jerry got on, although there wasn't any real evidence that Jerry was going to buy it. It could just belong to Mr. Overfield.

Mary said, "Hello, my name is Mary Fisher, and I'm doing research on the Cape Cod boat-brokering industry. I understand you're a good source?"

The woman said cheerfully, "Oh yes. Mr. Overfield has been number one in sales for the past three years running."

Number one in sales compared to whom? Mary wondered, but she didn't interrupt as the woman went on about the business, making it seem as if Mr. Overfield were the only boat broker of any credibility in the entire state of Massachusetts. Much of what she told Mary didn't seem relevant to her questions about Jerry, and she didn't feel comfortable bluntly asking the woman if she could give information about Mr. Overfield's clients.

"Mr. Overfield puts together an up-to-date packet of information about boats for sale," the woman said. "Would you like me to send it to you?"

"Sure, that would be great." Mary gave the woman the address of the shop to mail the packet of info. She wasn't entirely sure why she'd requested it, but perhaps it was good just to cover her bases.

"Thank you very much," Mary told the woman, feeling like she really hadn't gotten much useful information at all.

"No problem. Feel free to call again if you have any more questions."

The store phone rang. "Mary's Mystery Bookshop."

"Hi, Mrs. Fisher. This is Megan."

"Oh, hi, Megan. I hope you have good news for me?"

"I hope so. I think the problem is your motherboard."

Mary hesitated. "The what?"

"Sorry. It's a component of your laptop. It'll have to be replaced."

"Oh dear. How much will that cost?"

"Well, normally I wouldn't recommend replacing it because it's usually difficult to do. But this particular laptop motherboard isn't too hard to replace, and one of my fr—" Megan cut herself off. Then she continued, "One of the kids at my school's computer club has a dad who works for a retail store for your brand of computer. The store's about forty-five minutes away, but Bryan's dad always has parts and components lying around his house. I texted Bry, and he has a motherboard for your laptop model. It was from a refurbished laptop, but the computer was hardly used, and Bry says the motherboard's in great shape. Since it's from an old model, he says you can just have it for free. I can do the work. Would you be okay with that, even though it's not brand-new?"

"Of course. Free is so much better than buying a new computer. Thank you so much, Megan. And please tell Bryan thank you too."

"Sure. I'm going to bike to Bry's house to get the motherboard, and your computer should be ready in a couple of hours."

Mary hung up the phone, then did a little jig of elation. How wonderful that Megan could fix her computer! Her manuscript wasn't lost!

Something about Megan's voice had troubled her, however. She'd cut herself off when she said the word *friend*, and Mary wondered why. Did it have to do with the computer club at school or someone in particular? She didn't think it would be Bryan, if Megan was talking with him about her computer. Mary hoped Megan was doing all right.

Mary got a few customers in the hour that Rebecca was gone for her lunch break. Then it was Mary's turn to grab lunch.

As she walked out the door, she happened to look across the street and see Jayne smiling and waving off a happy customer who had apparently bought an antique lamp. Since Jayne was in a better frame of mind than this morning, Mary crossed the street to talk to her.

"Hi, Mary." Jayne smiled and opened her mouth as if to say something more, but then the phone in the shop rang. "Sorry. Give me a sec."

Mary followed Jayne inside her store and looked at the jewelry in the glass case as Jayne answered the phone. Then a strange tone in Jayne's voice caught Mary's attention.

"Yes, it is." Jayne spoke in a high, tight voice unlike normal. "Yes...yes... No, I'm afraid those are all the pictures I have...." Jayne turned slightly away from where Mary stood at the case so that her back was to her as she spoke on the phone.

Thinking Jayne wanted privacy, Mary wandered around, looking at the items for sale. She wasn't as into antiques as Betty was, but she still appreciated the lovely craftsmanship and old-world styling of the pieces. There was an antique quilt draped on a rack in the far corner next to a buffet table with elaborately carved feet, edges, and handles. On top rested several gorgeous lamps with scrollwork brass and beaded lampshades.

Next to all that was a tall antique clock. Mary remembered when Jayne bought it—she'd spoken to her the day it arrived in the shop. Jayne had been very excited about it and looked forward to selling it.

However, now there was a Not for Sale sign posted on it. Mary scrutinized the clock. At first, she thought it wasn't for sale because it was broken, but she could see that the mechanism was working and the time matched her watch. Had it already been sold? But if that were the case, Jayne would have put a Sold sign on the clock, not a Not for Sale sign.

"Certainly. What's your number?" Jayne spoke into the phone. It sounded like the conversation was winding down. "Thank you. Good-bye." As soon as the phone clicked into the cradle, Jayne called, "Oh, Mary, be careful...." Again, her voice had that high, tight quality that Mary hadn't heard before.

Mary turned to look at her and saw the anxiety in Jayne's eyes. She felt a bit like a child being scolded, but she tried to brush it off. "Oh, sorry, Jayne. It's a special piece, huh?"

Jayne tried to smile, but it didn't quite reach her eyes. "Oh, it's no big deal. I'm just a bit jumpy today. Don't mind me at all."

She returned to the counter where Jayne stood, and Mary's eyes fell on the pad of paper near the phone, upside down from Mary's angle, a pen lying next to it. She wouldn't have remarked on it if Jayne hadn't followed her gaze and made a jerky motion with her hand to hide the number on the pad.

How strange. That must be the number of the person who had just called. Mary slid a placid expression on her face as if she didn't notice Jayne's gesture. "I just wanted to see how you were doing today," Mary said with an intentionally pleasant smile, which she didn't normally have to force. "I was worried about you after what happened yesterday."

"Oh, that's nice, Mary. Thanks. I'm fine today. I was a little shaken yesterday, that's all."

Mary tried not to look at Jayne suspiciously. "I don't blame you. Anyone would be." She thought for a moment about how to draw out more information from Jayne without coming off as outright accusative. "Your spinning demonstration was such a hit, Jayne. Before yesterday, I never knew what flax fibers looked like."

Jayne's face flushed lightly with pride. "I learned how to spin from my grandmother, and she loved spinning flax. She usually spun strong rope or cords from the flax because that's what was needed around the house, but when she had time, she'd spin fine lace-weight linen yarn that she knitted into lace shawls. The linen becomes a lustrous yarn with lovely drape when it's knitted."

"How are you going to use the cord you spun at yesterday's demonstration?"

"Sandra asked to have it."

Mary's heart skipped a beat. "Sandra Rink? The teller at the bank?"

"Yes." Jayne's demeanor suddenly turned tight again. "I had been about to throw it away. It wasn't very well spun—it was uneven because I was talking while I was spinning and not focusing very well, but Sandra didn't seem to mind." Jayne shrugged, almost as if she were distracted by another thought. "I suppose she needed it for something."

"Maybe." It looked like Jayne was off the hook about the fibers, but Mary felt too close to connecting a dot in this mystery, so she couldn't help saying to Jayne, "See, the reason I ask is because, well, I happened to be behind the bank yesterday afternoon and saw some flax fibers on the ground. You didn't happen to go back there yesterday, did you?"

Mary watched Jayne closely to gauge her reaction, which was why she noticed when Jayne's eyes widened slightly and her skin paled. "Behind the bank? No, of course not." Her voice wobbled the tiniest bit.

Mary was confused. Was Jayne lying again? Her strange emotional reaction to Mary's question seemed to indicate she was. But why would she lie? First, denying that she'd been at the reenactment, and now this. Was it really Sandra who'd wanted the flax, or was Jayne making that up? And why would she have been behind the bank at all?

Jayne cleared her throat and seemed to regain her composure. "Why were you behind the bank? There isn't anything back there, is there?"

"Not really," Mary said, trying to keep a light tone. "The Courts' dog got loose."

"Oh yeah." Jayne's face cleared. "You found him?"

"Behind the bank." Mary didn't mention that Pipp was the reason for only the first time she went behind the bank yesterday, and not the second time. Mary remembered the man she'd seen Jayne talking to earlier in the alley. She was tempted to ask Jayne about him, but after Jayne's strange behavior just now, she thought it better not to say anything to her.

A customer walked into the store. Jayne automatically turned to look, and while Jayne was preoccupied, Mary stole a quick glance at the notepad near the phone at the counter and memorized the phone number.

"I'll see you later, Jayne," Mary said quickly.

"Thanks for coming by to check up on me." Then Jayne turned to smile at the customer.

Mary left the antique shop, but paused when she was out of sight of the door to hastily remove her notebook from her purse and write down the phone number. She reflected on the conversation with Jayne with some amazement. She'd sounded so odd while on the phone, and she'd tried to hide the phone number from Mary. Then Jayne had lied to her at least once, perhaps twice. Sweet Jayne Tucker, of all people. Why? Was Jayne somehow involved in the strange events surrounding the robbery? Mary couldn't see Jayne being involved in anything shady like that.

She'd said she'd given the linen rope to Sandra Rink. But Mary didn't quite understand why Sandra would have wanted Jayne's linen cord. Also, how likely was it that fibers happened to fall loose from her purse when the cord had been so tightly spun? And why behind the bank, the last place Steve had been seen?

One possibility jumped to Mary's mind, although she didn't like it. What if Jayne's cord had been used to tie someone up? Some fibers could have been pulled loose if someone were handling it to bind up someone or something. Steve was missing, and Mary suspected he hadn't been the robber in the bank. Did someone use the cord to tie Steve up? The thought chilled her.

And was Sandra somehow involved in it? She had been the one to ask Jayne for her cord yesterday, and she worked at the bank and knew about the reenactment. It seems obvious why she'd want Jayne's cord, *if she was guilty.*

But Mary couldn't shake the feeling that Jayne had lied to her. She might have been lying about giving the cord to Sandra. Or was it possible Jayne was working with Sandra? No, if she were, Jayne probably wouldn't have admitted to giving Sandra the cord.

But perhaps there was a simple, innocent reason for the flax fibers behind the bank. Maybe Mary could pay a visit to Sandra when she got off work at the end of the day to ask her about the linen rope.

There had to be a reasonable explanation for all of it. The alternative was that something had happened to Steve, and Mary just didn't want to think what that could be.

EIGHT

◆◆◆

Mary pushed open the door to the Tea Shoppe and was engulfed in a spicy fragrance that reminded her of pumpkin and apple pies. She glanced at the teacup-shaped chalkboard hanging above the counter and saw that the tea of the day was a pumpkin-spice chai tea, which sounded wonderful. Mary decided to get a cup to go.

The shop was rather full because it was lunchtime. Mary went to the refrigerated cooler in the corner to look at the premade deli sandwiches. She chose a club sandwich with turkey, bacon, lettuce, and tomato, and headed to the counter to pay for it.

As she stood in line, she noticed that there was a harried-looking waitress working the few tables scattered across the plank floors while the owner Sophie Mershon was at the cash register.

Deputy Wadell entered the shop, grabbed a sandwich, and got in line behind Mary. She gave him a friendly smile, and he nodded to her. "Hi, Mrs. Fisher. I'm glad I saw you, because I was going to call you this afternoon. It's about that book."

Mary's interest quickened. "You mean the historical book I lent to Steve Althorpe?"

"That's the one. That had the account of the original robbery, right? Chief McArthur sent me to search Mr. Althorpe's house again today, but I didn't find it. The chief said to make sure I told you."

"Thank you, Deputy. I appreciate you looking for it." Mary was heartened that the chief had taken her seriously enough to send Deputy Wadell to look for the book after she'd called him about it, although it got rid of her excuse to look through Steve's house. But now she wondered what happened to the book. Had Steve taken it with him? But why? Or had someone else—perhaps the true thief—taken the book? Was that how they knew what to do in the reenactment?

This all seemed very strange, and Mary wondered if she ought to spend more time finding out about the book, specifically. Maybe it had a clue to the robbery, after all. She knew a few other bookstore owners in the area. Perhaps one of them had a copy.

Mary finally made it to the front of the line, and Sophie greeted her with, "Sorry about the wait. Did you want anything besides the sandwich?"

"I'd love a cup of your tea special for today, to go."

"Sure thing, Mary." Sophie went to make the tea and came back to ring Mary's order up. She moved with extraordinary grace and a straight carriage, making it easy to believe that she'd once been a ballet dancer before coming to Ivy Bay to open her tea shop.

Mary paid for her sandwich and tea, and then Sophie topped off the paper to-go cup with a dollop of whipped cream before pressing a raised lid over it. "Enjoy!"

"Thanks, Sophie."

Mary sipped some of the fragrant chai as she walked. It was warm and comforting, transporting her back to memories of her house on Thanksgiving Day with the scent of pumpkin pies baking in the oven.

She still had a few minutes before she needed to be back at the store, and she wanted to get her thoughts down while they were still fresh. She headed to Albert Paddington Park.

She bypassed the whitewashed gazebo with its plaque commemorating the early settler Albert Paddington, who had donated the land for the park. She followed one of the many stone pathways that crisscrossed in front of the gazebo until she found an empty wooden bench sheltered by a tree on one side.

She pulled out her notebook and looked at the number she'd copied from Jayne's notepad. She was a little worried about invading Jayne's privacy, although the notepad had been out in the open, and Jayne hadn't cared enough about it to tear the page off the top and put it away. But Jayne's action of trying to cover it with her hand seemed odd as well as the fact she seemed to have been lying to Mary earlier.

Mary was torn. She didn't want to think that her suspicions about Jayne were really founded, but Jayne's actions seemed so odd that she couldn't ignore them. And if Jayne somehow, incredibly, did have something to do with the robbery and Steve's disappearance, Mary just couldn't stand by and not try to do something to investigate it.

Her decision made, she pulled out her cell phone and nervously dialed the number she'd copied from the notepad next to Jayne's telephone. The phone rang a few times. Then a man's voice answered, "Hello?"

"Hello, this is Mary Fisher. I'm calling about the phone conversation you had a little while ago with Jayne Tucker."

"Jayne Tucker?" His consonants were precise, his vowels slightly drawn out. He sounded almost like a butler.

"From Gems and Antiques store in Ivy Bay."

"Oh, that's right. This is about the antique clock for sale?"

The clock with the Not for Sale sign? The conversation was getting more interesting. "Yes," she said in a firm, businesslike tone to try to make it sound like she knew what she was talking about. "You're still interested in buying it, right?"

"Possibly," he drawled.

Hadn't Jayne mentioned something about there being no other pictures? "I'm calling about the pictures of the clock that you wanted."

"What about them?"

Mary hesitated, her mind whirling, remembering the snippet of conversation she'd overheard from Jayne. "Could you tell me again what other pictures you wanted?"

"I'm not sure, just…more." He sounded impatient.

Mary wasn't sure what he meant. Didn't the pictures he had already seen show the entire clock? "Are there specific angles missing? Or is there information you need?"

"Not *specific* angles, but the pictures on the Web site are kind of sparse."

Web site? Perhaps Jayne listed the clock online in an online auction. Mary knew that Jayne did that occasionally for some of her antiques. Or had she put it up on some other Web site somewhere?

Mary thought quickly. If it was an auction, there would be a deadline. "How soon do you need the pictures?" she asked him.

"Before the auction closes, obviously," the man said sarcastically.

Mary was right. The clock was listed on an online auction. But Jayne had said that those were all the pictures she had. Why would she say that when the clock was right in her store?

And why would she have a Not for Sale sign on it when she was selling it on an online auction? Was she not able to withdraw it from the auction if she sold it in person? But if someone came into the store and wanted the clock, Jayne could have just told the customer to bid on the auction. She could have even let the customer borrow her computer right there in the store.

"Look," the man said rudely, "if Jayne isn't going to get more pictures, then you're just wasting my time."

Mary wondered what photos he thought were missing. She'd have to find the online listing to see. "Okay, well, thank you for your time." She hung up.

After she hung up, she made more notes in the notebook she'd written in earlier: *Jayne was originally trying to sell the antique clock in her store, but now she has a Not for Sale sign on it. Why?*

It seemed Jayne was trying to sell the clock online or at an auction. Jayne once told Mary that while she did some online sales and auctions, she usually sold things for a higher price when people came into the store, because then she could talk to them about the particular items. She said she didn't do many online listings or auctions. So why was she promoting this clock online and not at the store? Or why wasn't she trying to sell the clock both online *and* at the store—wouldn't that be more likely to garner a faster sale?

She also remembered how Jayne had seemed nervous when Mary had been looking at the clock at the store. Mary had thought at the time that it was because Jayne had just got off the phone, and the phone conversation had seemed to make her a bit nervous, but what if she had spoken so sharply to Mary because of the clock?

What was going on with Jayne? It seemed like quite a stretch, but did this clock have something to do with the bank robbery? What if the robber had been targeting specific items that were stolen from the safe-deposit boxes and it somehow connected back to this clock and Jayne? Or was that too far-fetched an idea?

Well, she didn't have access to a list of what had been stolen, but she did have these clues to follow. She had to make sure she spoke to Sandra later today about Jayne's linen rope.

Mary had been waiting for Megan to call about her laptop when the phone finally rang midafternoon. "Hello, Mary's Mystery Bookshop."

"Hi, Mrs. Fisher. It's Megan." Megan's voice had a doleful note that didn't bode well. "I guess I don't know what's wrong with your computer after all."

"It wasn't the... motherboard?"

"Well, I thought it was at first. But I replaced it, and the computer's still not working. I think you'll need to take it to a *real* computer technician to fix it." The way Megan said the word *real* gave Mary the impression that Megan wasn't just frustrated and disappointed, but that this failure might have hit at her self-esteem.

"I'll come by right now, if that's okay?" Mary said.

"Sure, Mrs. Fisher."

Mary hung up and turned to Rebecca. "I'm going to go pick up my laptop from Megan's house."

"Okay. Is it fixed?"

Mary shook her head.

Rebecca gave her a sympathetic look. "While you're gone, I'll look up that computer-repair shop I used before."

"Thanks, Rebecca."

Mary walked to Megan's house since it was closer than walking home, getting her car, and driving there. She had just reached the front door when Megan opened it. Instead of the confident young woman she'd been this morning, her shoulders slumped and she looked like a deflated balloon.

"I'm so sorry, Mrs. Fisher. I really thought the new motherboard was the answer."

"I know you did your best, and that's all I asked for."

"Your computer's here." Megan led the way to the living room, where Mary's laptop sat on the coffee table. "I just don't understand," she said, glowering at the laptop. She shook her blue-streaked bangs out of her eyes.

Mary sat next to Megan on the couch. "What exactly did you do?" Mary asked, even though she knew she wouldn't understand a word of the answer.

Megan's words rushed out of her in frustration, and she rattled on about "PC beeps," "power supply," "POST card," "motherboard," and "power button."

Megan hit the power button on the laptop, and it powered on, then powered off.

"Well, that's new," Mary said. "Before, it didn't even power on."

Megan froze. "Hey, you're right. When you brought it in, it didn't power up at all." She stared hard at the computer, but her gaze was unfocused. Then her eyes lit up. "That's it! I think I know what's wrong...."

Megan took the laptop, unplugged it, and began unscrewing and dismantling it. Mary's heart just about stopped as she saw Megan scatter the hard-shell case and screws and undefinable pieces of computer all over the coffee table.

"Okay, battery's out...." Megan opened a compartment and took out two sticks of metal about the size of sticks of gum. She grabbed one and replaced it back in the computer, then reassembled everything, but without one of the metal sticks.

"You...forgot that piece," Mary said.

"That's on purpose." Megan flipped the laptop over and then hit the power button. "Let's hope it's the right RAM stick."

Immediately, the hard drive whirred, and the screen came on. Mary held her breath, and then the computer began its normal start-up procedure.

"You did it!" In her excitement, Mary gave Megan's thin shoulders a quick squeeze.

Megan just shrugged, but a pleased pink blossomed in her cheeks. "I should have thought of that before. Then I wouldn't have worried you."

Mary looked at the little metal stick still lying on the coffee table. "So that was the problem?"

"Actually, your motherboard *was* the main problem, but it hadn't occurred to me that one of your RAM sticks would also be defective."

"RAM sticks?" Mary had visions of sheep with sticks in their mouths, even though she knew that couldn't be what Megan was talking about.

"They're your computer's memory. Your computer will run with only one, but it'll be slow unless you replace this one."

"Where can I get one?"

"Anywhere. They're cheap. But I can ask Bryan if he has one lying around that he can give me. He's always upgrading his RAM, so he might have one he doesn't want."

"Your friend is so kind."

"Oh, he's not my friend...." Megan trailed off, and her eyes clouded.

Mary touched Megan's hand. "You said something like that before. Did you two have a fight or something?"

"It's complicated." She looked away, frowning.

"Sometimes it's good to talk about it with someone who's not involved in the situation. Maybe they can give you good advice."

Megan stared at the wall and then her shoes. "It's no big deal. I just don't belong to the computer club at school anymore."

"Why not?"

"Some of them are getting into illegal hacking. They like the challenge, or maybe they just like being rebellious. But I don't want to do that, and they don't understand why."

Mary nodded sagely. "I think you're very brave to stand up for what you believe in. It must be pretty hard for you at school, then."

Megan's brows wrinkled. "I feel like I've lost all my friends. I guess I have. All my friends belong to computer club."

"Like Bryan?"

Megan nodded. "I don't fit in anywhere. I love computers, and I thought I'd found a place to belong with the computer club, but now..."

Mary remembered the intricacies of high school, both when she was a teenager and also in helping her kids through their teen years. "It must be lonely for you to not have a group to belong to. But aren't there other groups you could join?"

Megan shrugged. "Like what?"

"What other things do you like doing?"

"Just computers. That's all I've ever really liked." Megan's voice wobbled.

Mary squeezed her hand. "I'm positive that a smart young girl like you is much more multifaceted. Oops, I used an SAT word."

Megan snorted.

"I think we just need to be creative and think of other options for you. We need to think out of the box."

"But... the only place a computer geek belongs is in the computer club."

"First of all, you're not a geek or a nerd. No such language around me. As far as I'm concerned, you're a computer *wizard*. A computer *genius*."

Megan gave a small smile.

"There, that's better. I'll think about the problem, and you will too. We'll think of some other options for you at school, some other clubs you might enjoy, new people to form friendships with."

Megan nodded, but she didn't look convinced.

"In the meantime," Mary continued, "why don't you help me out?"

"But your computer's fixed already."

"I mean, use your computer genius on something that's been bothering me. My friend Jayne is selling an antique clock online somewhere, but I don't know where. I tried searching online this afternoon before you called, but I came up with nothing. I'm wondering if she's using a different name. Do you think you could find out for me?"

"Of course. But…you didn't want to just ask Mrs. Tucker?"

"I could, but"—Mary gave Megan a wink—"think of it as online sleuthing, but without the illegal-hacking part."

Megan's eyes brightened. "Okay. I'm game."

"Great. I'll leave you to it. And keep it between you and me, okay?"

"You got it. I'll call you when I find it."

Mary left Megan's house to walk back to the shop, glad she'd thought of this task to help Megan feel more confident in herself. Mary assumed she'd be able to find the online auction herself, but it would take her longer than it would take Megan, who was adept at computers and more comfortable on the Internet than she was. Mary couldn't help but think that this clock was somehow connected to Jayne's strange behavior about the bank and the things she had been lying about.

It still seemed beyond ludicrous that Jayne would be involved in anything shady, though. Surely there was a simple explanation for all of this.

NINE

If Mary hadn't decided to walk down Liberty Road to get back to her store, she wouldn't have thought of it. But as she approached the corner of Liberty and Meeting House Road, her eyes fell on the library, and she had a flash of inspiration.

Originally, she'd used the historical book she'd lent Steve as an excuse to try to search his house, and only after finding out the book was missing did she realize that maybe she should try to find another copy of it. She'd briefly thought about asking other bookstore owners she knew, but why not see if the library had a copy?

Mary eagerly headed toward the redbrick building and entered through the white front doors. Inside was warmer than the outside temperature but not uncomfortably so, and the skylights in the high, vaulted ceiling filled the room with the fall sunlight, making it seem more like summertime.

The librarian Victoria Pickerton was at the front desk, and she looked up when Mary entered the library. "Hi, Mary," she said with a wide smile. Her cat's-eye glasses today were a brilliant scarlet that matched the colors on the autumn leaves.

"Hi, Victoria. How are you doing?"

"Feeling like I'd like to curl up in an armchair by a window with a good book today!" Victoria laughed. "The weather's fantastic."

Mary nodded agreement. "Did you get to go to any of Living History Day yesterday?"

"Definitely. The other library workers and I traded off time so we could go to the demonstrations we wanted to see. I caught some of the moccasin making and the fashion show. I caught the tail end of your bookbinding demonstration too, but I was near the back of the crowd."

"I was so nervous doing that," Mary said. "Until I did the research for it, I hadn't realized how elaborate the process was. When I was a librarian, I mostly repaired books—I didn't have to assemble one from scratch."

"We don't often do the entire bookbinding process either, but I have repaired my fair share of books," Victoria said with a roll of her eyes.

At that moment, a patron came up with some books and a question about a title, so Mary waved to Victoria and headed toward the computers that housed the library catalog and sat down. But as she poised her hands over the keyboard, she suddenly realized she didn't remember the title of the book she'd lent to Steve.

She could see the cover in her mind's eye. She'd received the box of books, and the crude drawing of Elias Cowper glared out at her under the word *Wanted* from the antique poster. But what had the title been?

Something about gold—no, silver. Silver tongue! That's what it had been. *A Silver-Tongued Thief.* She typed it into the computer, and it immediately gave her *A Silver-Tongued*

Thief: A Story of Violence and Crime by Emmanuel Brockett. Mary wrote the number on a piece of paper and moved to the stacks to find the book.

She wandered for a while among the blond-oak bookcases, passing occasional cozy nooks and reading areas, some empty and some with patrons engrossed in books. She finally found the bookshelves she wanted and ran her finger down the book spines, looking for the right title.

Wait a minute; it wasn't there. She looked through the books more carefully. Had she mistaken the number? She looked at the number she'd written down. Maybe she'd transcribed it wrong.

She went all the way back to the computer and double-checked, but it was the correct number. And the computer catalog said clearly that the book was on the shelves.

Confused, she returned to the shelf. Perhaps the book had been misshelved? She looked through all the books on the shelf, noting that in the area the book should have been were other historical stories about thieves and murderers. She must be in the right area, but the book wasn't there. She also realized that if the book was misshelved, it could be anywhere in the entire library. She checked the titles anyway, in case it had only been misplaced on the same bookcase. No luck.

She sighed. She needed to talk to Victoria.

She headed to the front desk and was surprised to see Patricia Avakian, Jerry's wife, holding a stack of books while waiting in line.

"Hi, Patricia," Mary said.

Patricia turned to see Mary, and she could have sworn she saw alarm flash briefly across Patricia's eyes. "Hi, Mary." Patricia smiled, but the greeting seemed a bit lukewarm.

How odd. Was the reaction because of Mary specifically, or was there something bothering Patricia?

Then she saw Patricia juggle the stack of books and try to surreptitiously slip some books from the bottom of the stack onto the top. Just idle shuffling of her books or deliberate?

"Looks like you've got quite the research project," Mary prompted.

"Oh no. Just novels." Patricia grabbed one book from the bottom and held it up. "Historical fiction is my favorite." Then she put the book back on the top of the stack.

The woman in front of Patricia finished her business and walked away, and Patricia quickly went up to the counter to speak to Victoria.

"Hi, Victoria," Patricia said. "I was looking for a historical novel, *Veil of Pearls* by MaryLu Tyndall? Is the library going to get it?" She slid her stack of books onto the counter next to her, tilted her head ever so slightly away from Mary, and shifted the stack so the titles weren't readily visible.

"How do you spell that?" Victoria asked as she turned to her computer behind the desk.

Mary tried easing her way to the side to try to see the spines of the books, but Patricia's body blocked her view, either innocently or deliberately.

Finally, Victoria pointed to her computer and said, "Here it is. It's been ordered, and it should arrive at the library sometime next week. I can call you once I've processed it."

"That would be great." Patricia gave Victoria her phone number.

Victoria then pulled the books behind the counter toward her so she could check the books out for Patricia. Mary couldn't see over the counter at the titles, but after the librarian was done, Patricia grabbed her stack of books, preparing to leave.

As Patricia moved away from the counter with her books in her arms, Mary glanced at the spines quickly. They were mostly historical novels, but Mary's eyes immediately picked out the only title that stood out among the other novels: *Boats A–Z*.

However, when Patricia saw Mary looking at her books, she clutched the books closer to her and shifted the stack so that the spines were hidden.

"See you, Mary." Patricia headed to the door.

Victoria smiled at Mary. "Hey, there, stranger, we need to stop meeting like this. Looks like you need my help with something?"

Mary had almost forgotten what she had been standing in line for. "I'm looking for this book, but it's not in the stacks. I checked the entire bookcase, and it's missing." Mary gave her the title and author and the number she'd copied down.

Victoria checked on her computer. "It should be on the shelf, and if it isn't, then it's missing."

Mary's heart sank. "Is there anything you can do?"

"I can order another copy. It should be here in a week or two."

That might be too late. Mary would need to see if she could contact other bookstore owners to get a copy sooner, but in case that didn't pan out, she figured a week or two was better than nothing. "Yes, could you please do that?"

"Of course." Victoria ordered the book online while Mary was standing there. "I'll call you when it's in."

"Thanks." But instead of leaving right away, Mary went back to the computer library catalog and looked up *Boats A–Z*. She found the listing as *Boats A–Z: Buying, Sailing, Selling Your Boat*.

Mary thought back to Jerry's reference to money in his intense discussion with Steve just before the robbery. She also remembered him speaking to Gibson Overfield, a boat broker, just as they were climbing into a very nice boat. Was Jerry buying that nice boat? Was that why Patricia was checking out this book from the library?

She wasn't entirely sure how Jerry had gotten the funds to buy a boat—perhaps he'd saved up for it. But the book Patricia borrowed seemed to show that Jerry's wife also knew about the boat.

Mary paused to wonder if perhaps she was meddling too much. Perhaps she shouldn't get involved at all in the Avakians' business.

But what if they did have something to do with Steve's disappearance and the robbery? Could she really stand by and do nothing when Steve might be in danger?

But the police could handle the investigation, surely. She had great faith in Chief McArthur and his officers. Wouldn't Mary just be getting in their way?

But the police had to adhere to their procedures, and they didn't have the proof to follow up with the things Mary had a gut instinct about. Her instinct had been right often in the past. If the police couldn't or wouldn't follow up on these things, shouldn't Mary do a little gentle probing? Especially if that's all it was, sensitive and considerate questions that were in no way invasive.

Mary didn't know Jerry very well, but she felt she could speak to Patricia a little easier than Jerry. If Mary could get a chance to speak to Patricia alone, maybe Mary could find out what was going on. Maybe Patricia could shed some light on the boat they were buying, and even the argument she'd overheard between Jerry and Steve.

Mary couldn't help thinking that the Avakians buying a boat was coincidental timing, right when a lot of valuables and money were missing from the bank.

On the walk from the library back to the bookstore, Mary could smell the faint scent of wood smoke from a fireplace that undercut the tang of the sea. The sun still shone on the fall day, and Mary guessed someone couldn't resist a fire even though winter hadn't yet settled in and it wasn't quite frigid enough to need one.

When Mary returned to her bookstore, Rebecca met her with a note scribbled on a piece of paper. "Megan called while you were gone. She asked if you could please call her back."

Mary was surprised. Had Megan already found the online listing for the antique clock? She glanced at the note and saw that it wasn't Megan's home phone number. She dialed, and Megan answered.

"Hi, Mrs. Fisher. Are you free right now?"

"Sure. I can come by your house—"

"Actually, I biked downtown. I wanted to go to the store to look at that clock."

"Oh, that's a good idea. It hadn't occurred to me that you didn't know what it looked like."

"I might've made Mrs. Tucker a little nervous when I went into the store, but I told her I was looking around for a Christmas present for my mom, which was perfectly true. I just didn't find anything there she'd like."

Mary remembered the modern feel of Megan's house. "Your mom doesn't care for antiques?"

"Nope."

"Where are you now?"

"The ice-cream parlor."

"I'll meet you there." Mary hung up and glanced at Rebecca.

She didn't even have to ask her question because Rebecca laughed and said, "I'll mind the shop."

"I'm glad we're not too busy, or I wouldn't dream of leaving you to handle the crowd all by yourself."

Mary hurried across and then down Main Street toward Bailey's Ice Cream Shop. She immediately saw Megan seated at one of the small, white wrought-iron tables with a laptop in front of her and a backpack on the floor at her feet. Also, Mary's computer laptop case was draped over the back of her chair. Next to her was an empty ice-cream cup and spoon.

"Hi, Mrs. Fisher," Megan said. "Hey, I got your flavor of the month, and it was really good."

Bailey's featured a new flavor of Mary's every month, and this time Mary had given Tess Bailey a recipe for pumpkin-spice ice cream with maple chips and pieces of graham-cracker crust mixed in. Mary had worked hard to make sure the pumpkin flavor was subtle and not overpowering, and she thought the maple-syrup chips and graham-cracker crust pieces added nice texture.

Mary sat at a chair at the table. "I'm glad you liked it. I used to make something like this for my kids every Halloween."

Megan reached down beside her chair and grabbed Mary's laptop case, handing it over to her. "It still doesn't have a new memory stick in it. I'll put it in for you tomorrow."

"Does it work?"

"Oh yeah. It'll just run kinda slow until I replace the RAM stick." Megan turned the laptop toward Mary. "I think I found the listing for the clock."

"How in the world did you do it?"

Megan grinned. "I felt like a spy or something. Mrs. Tucker used a fake name, and I had to figure out what her alternate profile ID would be."

There was the clock on the Web site Megan had found. It was an antique online auction site, and the seller profile ID was RedheadRegina. "I understand the redhead part, but who's Regina?"

"That's Mrs. Tucker's middle name."

"How did you find that?"

"I looked her up and found she's on some antique forum boards. I found a profile page for her—it had her store Web site on the page—and it said that her middle name was Regina."

"Clever."

Megan looked pleased. "Thanks. Then I searched for Regina on a bunch of Web sites selling and found the profile for RedheadRegina. I did some digging and found an IP address for her and traced it back to the physical address of the shop. As soon as I saw the clock in the store, I knew RedheadRegina was her."

Mary was impressed. It would have taken her a bit longer to think of trying to find Jayne's middle name for an alternate profile ID, and Mary definitely would have had to spend valuable time doing research to figure out about IP addresses and finding a person's location.

Mary saw the price of the clock and frowned. The price for the clock was lower than the price Jayne had bought it for. She'd spoken to Jayne when the clock arrived in the store, and she had told Mary she'd gotten it for a good deal. This price was several hundred dollars less than what she paid for it.

Jayne had covered the phone number of the potential auction bidder, and she'd put up that Not for Sale sign, which made Mary suspect Jayne wanted to somehow hide the fact she was selling the clock online. But why? And why for less than what she bought it for? The only clue that she had was this clock. Mary needed to find out more about it.

"Isn't it the same clock?" Megan looked anxious, and Mary immediately erased her frown.

"It's the clock, all right. You're brilliant! I'm amazed you found the listing so quickly."

"It was fun, actually." Megan looked happier than she'd been since Mary saw her at Living History Day—her eyes sparkled again, and she had that lift of confidence in her chin.

"I'm glad. I was hoping this wasn't too boring for you. I'm sure there are more exciting ways for you to spend your fall break."

"Are you kidding? This was like a game. Plus, like you said, I knew it wasn't anything illegal."

Mary felt a rush of satisfaction that she might have helped Megan feel a bit better about herself. She wished she could do something more to help Megan's situation at school. She'd have to keep her eye open for things she could say or do to help encourage the young teen.

The ice-cream shop was starting to get crowded with a wave of people coming in, despite the crisp fall weather. "Let's let someone else have this table," Mary said, rising to her feet and putting the laptop in its case.

Outside the ice-cream shop, Mary waved good-bye to Megan and headed back to the store.

As she was about to open the front door of the bookshop, she glanced at the bank across the street and saw the man in the suit and expensive wool coat whom she'd seen earlier that morning. He and Owen Cooper were standing just outside the front doors of the bank, as if they had been walking inside at the same time but their conversation had waylaid them. They both seemed very earnest, and Owen looked concerned.

Mary's gut twisted. What would all this mean for the bank? Would it indeed close because of the robbery? Or was it already slated for closure like so many other banks owned by Neels?

Mary wondered if there was a way to know for certain if this man was from the Neels Banking Group, but outside of accosting the man herself or asking Owen directly, which would be gossipy and which he probably couldn't say anything about anyway, she couldn't think of anything. Besides, it was the bank's business, not hers, and she instead needed to focus on finding out what happened to Steve and the missing items from the robbery.

Owen and the man then turned and entered the bank, but Mary suddenly had a realization. What if this man was an accountant, and he was here in Ivy Bay not to look at the bank's financials, but to find Jayne's missing funds? What if they weren't missing but stolen somehow? If things with Jayne's money were serious enough to bring in an accountant to look into the missing deposit, would it motivate whoever had stolen it to try to do something about it, like stage a robbery? The robbery could have been a distraction, or the items stolen from the safe-deposit boxes could have somehow had something to do with the bank.

Mary continued inside the store and, as she saw Rebecca, she said, "I just saw that man from Neels outside the bank."

"The one in the suit and wool coat? I saw him grab a sandwich from the Tea Shoppe at lunch. I tried saying hello, but he looked almost offended I'd talked to him. I think I scared him." Rebecca giggled. "He left as soon as he'd paid and headed straight back to the bank."

"He might be just focused on whatever reason he's here."

"You're probably right."

Mary went to the back to get herself a cup of tea, and while she was waiting for the water to boil, she thought about Jayne's missing funds. A week ago, Mary had overheard Jayne speaking to Steve about her missing money. Sandra had been the one who accepted Jayne's checks, and when Jayne realized the money wasn't in her account, she went back to the bank to talk to Steve. Would Jayne possibly be so upset about the missing money—especially if it was a very large sum—

that she'd do something crazy like partner with someone like Steve to rob the bank?

The thought seemed terribly wrong to Mary. It would be completely out of character for Jayne to do anything of the sort.

But she had to admit that Jayne had a reason to bear a grudge against the bank. And even more important, in light of the rumors that it was closing, Jayne might fear she'd never get her funds back. Mary wondered once again if the missing funds had something to do with the clock, although she couldn't for the life of her think of what.

If her missing funds were a large enough amount, would the situation with the bank make her desperate enough?

No. Surely not Jayne.

Mary remembered the flax fibers behind the bank and wondered if Jayne would partner with Sandra. No, because if she had, she wouldn't have blithely told Mary she'd given the rope to Sandra.

Mary sighed. This was all pure speculation, and she was starting to think in circles. She needed to look into the solid things she had—the questions surrounding the clock. She made a mental note to ask Betty about the antique clock and do her own research into it tonight.

TEN

—◆◆—

After Rebecca had left for home with Ashley, Mary closed up the shop but didn't head home herself. Instead, she went across the street to the bank and entered. Gus was safe in his carrier, and she hoped he wouldn't make a sound and give away the fact that she was carrying him into the bank.

The police had blocked the bank off for most of yesterday, collecting evidence, and while they'd cleared the bank to open today, there was a stray scrap of yellow Do Not Cross police tape on the floor, evidence of the investigation yesterday. The bank was empty, and Owen Cooper sat at Steve's desk.

Owen's shoulders slumped as he wrote something on a piece of paper, and he had his head in his hand. There was no sign of the man she assumed was the Neels banker—perhaps he was in the offices in back, or maybe he'd already left for the day. There also was no trace of Sandra.

"Hello, Owen," Mary said to her neighbor, and he looked up at her.

"Oh, hello, Mary." He sounded surprised to see her, as if it were an odd occurrence for someone to enter the bank. Perhaps it had been, today.

"Are you doing all right?" Mary sat on the other side of the lead banker's desk, in the chair set up across from Owen.

He sighed. "As well as can be expected, I suppose."

"I'm so sorry. I suppose the police haven't found Steve yet?"

"No. I just..." He sighed again. "I can't believe it of him. I feel betrayed."

"You don't know for certain if he did it. The police only suspect him and want to question him."

"I think it's a foregone conclusion that he's guilty. Who else could it be?"

Mary had to concede that he had a point, but she wasn't ready to give up on Steve. She also needed to talk to Sandra about the rope Jayne had given to her and the flax fibers behind the bank.

Owen continued, "We're not very busy right now, so if you need something, I'm completely at your disposal." He tried to smile, but it looked a bit sad.

"Oh, I just wanted to talk to Sandra. She was pretty shaken yesterday after talking to the police, and I gave her a cup of tea in my store to calm her. I want to make sure she's all right." That, and try to get some more information from her.

"I sent her home early," Owen said.

"Is she all right?" Mary asked, a little alarmed.

"She's okay. She was a bit quiet all day today," Owen said. "She and Steve worked closely together. This is as hard for her to take in as it is for me."

"Perhaps you should go home too," Mary suggested as she rose to her feet. "Tomorrow might look better. And I'll be praying for you."

"I appreciate that, Mary."

As Mary walked back to her bookstore, she said a silent prayer. *Dear Lord, please help everything go well for Owen and Sandra and the bank. He seems rather down, so please encourage him. And I pray that Steve is all right. Lord, please be with Megan right now too.*

Mary unlocked the front door to her bookshop and headed straight to the counter. Behind the counter in one of the cubbyholes was the town's telephone book.

She set it on the marble countertop and flipped through to the Rs. Ried, Riley, Rink. There it was: a listing for S. Rink. She was certain it was Sandra. Mary wrote down the address and put away the phone book. She had a map at home, and besides, she wanted to get her car.

Mary walked home and found Betty stretched out on the living room sofa, reading the latest issue of *Cape Cod Living* with a cup of tea near at hand. "How was your day?" Mary asked as she released Gus from the carrier.

"I had a few meetings, and then I worked in the garden when I came home rather than putting my feet up," Betty said. "So I'm doing that now."

"I have an errand I have to run before dinner," Mary said. "Did you want me to make you something to eat before I head out?"

"No, I'll just heat up some soup, and there's still deli meat for a sandwich. I'll be fine."

Mary got their map and then drove to Sandra's neighborhood, a little ways past Beacon Inn, where there were more residential homes along the street. She turned off on Agate Way, a small, quiet street lined with several duplexes, each with a quaint little front lawn. Some duplexes had vegetable gardens; others had bushes and flowers.

Mary found Sandra's duplex almost at the end of the street. Light glowed from the front window, which was covered by a cheerful blue-patterned curtain. The other side of the duplex was dark and the driveway empty—Sandra's neighbors weren't home. The house had recently been painted pale blue with darker blue trim, and Sandra's tiny front lawn contained only neatly trimmed grass. Her neighbors, on the other hand, had several large rosebushes.

Mary parked along the street in front of Sandra's front lawn and walked up the short concrete driveway past Sandra's car. As she approached the front door, however, she heard Sandra's voice.

She picked up only a couple of phrases: "I'm tired of bailing you out" and "You can't make me help you." That last made Mary pause. Was Sandra all right? Who was she talking to? A friend? A family member? Was she alone or on the phone? Mary thought she heard a man's deep murmur answer Sandra, but she couldn't be certain. If a man was there, he was speaking low.

Mary was suddenly made aware that she didn't know that much about Sandra's personal life. Sandra always greeted Mary cheerfully when she came into the bank, and when Mary asked her how she was doing, she always said fine with a smile that seemed genuine. But Mary didn't know anything about Sandra's family or friends. She knew Sandra was single and lived alone—Sandra might have mentioned that, or perhaps someone else in Ivy Bay had mentioned it to Mary—but other than that, she didn't know who Sandra hung out with or who her friends might be. Then again, Mary didn't hang out at the same events and places that a young single woman and her friends would hang out at, so perhaps it wasn't so surprising that Mary didn't see Sandra outside of the bank.

Mary didn't want to interrupt Sandra if she was talking to someone, but after a moment, Sandra's voice died away, so Mary knocked on the front door.

Sandra didn't open it right away, but when she did, she looked slightly agitated. At least until she saw Mary standing there. Then she lifted her eyebrows in surprise. "Oh. Hi, Mary."

"I hope you don't mind my stopping by, but I wanted to make sure you were all right."

Sandra smiled at her, and she seemed touched by Mary's concern. "That's sweet of you, Mary. Come on in."

Mary entered the apartment, walking straight into a charming little living room with an oak coffee table and a floral-patterned couch that looked comfy enough to drown happily in. She was immediately struck by the faint scent of cigarette smoke, but not the normal cigarette smell she was used to. This was different in a way she couldn't quite define, like a combination of tobacco and something sweeter. "I hope I haven't come at a bad time. I thought I heard you talking to someone as I walked up."

Mary wasn't sure if it was the low lighting coming only from the white brocade-covered lamps on the two small round end tables, but it seemed Sandra's face paled.

"Oh no. I was just on the phone," Sandra said quickly in a hoarse voice.

Her hoarseness was explained a second later when she coughed, grabbing a tissue from the tissue box on the coffee table to hold to her mouth.

"Are you all right?" Mary asked.

"Just allergies," Sandra said. "Have a seat. Can I get you some tea? I was just going to make a pot."

"If you're going to make some anyway, I'd love a cup."

Sandra went through an open doorway into a small kitchen just off the living room. Mary could see her refrigerator against the far wall, with some photos attached to the door.

Mary peered around the living room and noticed that the windows were all wide open despite the cool night air. To compensate for the chill, Sandra had lit a cozy fire in the small fireplace, and the smell of burning wood mingled with that odd cigarette scent. She hadn't known Sandra smoked— she never smelled of cigarettes, but then again, it could be that she smoked outside the bank and brushed her teeth afterward.

Mary glanced over the mantel of the fireplace, but there were only small glass art statues, no pictures. As she glanced down, she saw a trash can near the fireplace and the partially crumpled remains of a pack of cigarettes. She realized that the smell was odd because it was a different type of cigarette from the typical ones she'd seen—Veryan Chapp kretek cigarettes. Mary didn't know the type, but the package was a distinctive gold, green, and blue pattern.

Next to the trash can was a faded blue duffel bag, partially unzipped. Mary peeked inside and saw some extremely worn jeans and a couple of T-shirts and sweatshirts that looked rather ratty, with fraying at the necklines and a slightly grayish tinge from multiple washings. It was very unlike the neat, fashionable style Mary had always seen Sandra in. Even now, in lounging around her house,

Sandra wore a comfortable top and cotton stretch pants that looked well cared for. Mary looked closer, and she could see the brand of the jeans and also the tag on one of the sweatshirts, which indicated they belonged to a man, not a woman.

Sandra walked in with a tray, carrying the teapot, cups, and milk and sugar, and Mary sat on an overstuffed chair kitty-corner to the sofa. As she sat, her eyes fell on the corner of the coffee table where a pearl-and-gold earring lay.

"Is this the earring you wore yesterday?" Mary asked, picking it up.

"Yes, it's made by Nanine," Sandra said, naming a beloved local artisan.

"Oh, I love her. And this piece is lovely, but where's the other one?" Mary ducked down to look under the table, thinking it had fallen.

"I don't know. I lost it somewhere," Sandra said with a wrinkle between her brows. She seemed a little distracted, however, as she spoke and poured the tea.

"What a shame. I'd be disappointed to lose such a unique piece." Mary sat back with the fragrant cup, inhaling the scent of chamomile. "I noticed the incredible glass art statues on your fireplace. You have such an eye for the creative."

Sandra smiled, relaxing in Mary's compliment. "Thanks."

"Where did you get them?" Mary looked back at the glass statues on the fireplace, but found herself drawn again to the duffel bag of men's things.

Looking back at Sandra, and trying to think of polite conversation other than the obvious question about the bag, Mary realized that Sandra had followed her gaze to the duffel bag. Sandra's hand shook as she took a sip of the tea. Something was definitely off here.

Mary nodded toward the duffel bag near the fireplace. "Is someone staying with you? No need to be embarrassed about their stuff lying around. I find it's never easy to keep up with houseguests." She tried to sound sympathetic to put the other woman at ease. What woman didn't worry what others thought of them having things out of place?

Sandra looked at the duffel bag, and her eyes widened slightly. "That's my, um, workout bag. No one's staying with me."

Mary had the odd feeling that Sandra was lying. But why would she do that? There certainly wasn't any shame in having someone staying with her.

"Oh," Mary said lightly. "I'm sorry. I didn't mean to presume."

Sandra's lips thinned into a sort of smile, at least that's what Mary thought she was trying to do, but it looked more like a grimace. Mary took a sip of her tea. "This is delicious. What kind is it?"

As Sandra opened her mouth to answer, she began coughing furiously.

"Are you sure you're all right?" Mary asked when the coughing fit subsided.

"Yes." Sandra waved her off. "Just something in the air making my allergies act up."

"It smells a little like cigarette smoke in here. I hope someone didn't come over and make your house uncomfortable for you."

Sandra's eyes slid away from Mary's. "No, that's not it. I smoke occasionally. I recently picked it up again."

Mary looked at Sandra for a while. Something about this seemed wrong, but she shook it off. "There I go again, presuming. I'm so sorry."

Mary couldn't shake the feeling that something wasn't right with this situation. Still, she wasn't here to question Sandra's smoking habit. She'd come today to find out about the linen rope and to make sure Sandra was okay after everything that happened, not make the poor girl feel worse.

Mary set her teacup down and smiled at the younger woman. "I saw Owen at the bank this afternoon. I hope things weren't too bad today."

"I didn't have to deal with many people. I feel badly for Mr. Cooper because he had to handle everyone who came in to complain." The color hadn't returned to Sandra's face, even though she'd taken a few sips of tea. Perhaps the ordeal had shaken her more than Mary had imagined.

Mary shook her head. "This is terrible. Just when the bank needs the community to support it, people are getting upset."

"I feel awful about what happened," Sandra said.

"I think everyone's more shocked than anything else. Who would have thought Steve would do something like that?"

"I hope he's all right." Sandra's hands tightened around her teacup. "If he's guilty, I hope the police can bring him in soon, but if he's not, I hope they find out what happened to him."

Mary looked at Sandra carefully. Sandra was not only incredulous about what happened, but she seemed to have taken it a step farther than anyone else Mary had talked to and seemed anxious that Steve not be locked up. "You think there's a possibility Steve didn't rob the bank?"

"Well, the robber was masked, wasn't he? And it seems so incredible that Steve would do something like this—" Sandra broke off to cough a little.

Maybe it was best to change the subject. At least slightly. "It put a damper on Living History Day, didn't it?" Mary said. "Did you get to enjoy the other demonstrations yesterday at all?"

"Not really. Steve let me go to see a few things in the morning, but after the robbery, I just wanted to go home."

"That's a shame. At least you got to see Jayne Tucker's spinning demonstration. Jayne mentioned she gave you the linen rope she spun that day."

"Oh...Yes, I saw that one." Instead of being happy about seeing what Mary thought was one of the best demonstrations of the day, Sandra looked like she'd rather go hide in the teapot than talk about it. Which highlighted what had been bothering Mary.

"I'm glad Jayne had someone who wanted to take that linen rope off her hands." Mary gave a jovial laugh, hoping her lightheartedness would catch Sandra off guard. After all, she wasn't a police officer. Sandra had no reason to hide the information from her. "What in the world are you going to do with the silly thing?"

Sandra froze, almost as if she'd been turned to stone. Then she blinked, and she said in a hoarse voice, "I don't—" She broke off to cough a little, then continued, "I don't—" Her voice was even hoarser than before, and she fell into a bout of coughing. Her teacup started sloshing, so Mary took it from her and put it on the coffee table.

Mary hovered anxiously, wondering if Sandra was all right. Maybe she'd been wrong to even ask about the rope.

Sandra finally stopped coughing and said, "I'm afraid I don't remember what I did with it."

Maybe Mary was being paranoid about this, but what had Sandra needed the rope for?

"I was hoping to look at it again, if you had it," Mary said. "You didn't drop the rope somewhere? The parking lot, or behind the bank?" Mary asked, feeling slightly guilty that she already knew the answer, but hoped Sandra had nothing to do with it.

Sandra straightened. "No, I don't think so. Why would I go behind the bank?"

With what she hoped was a guileless expression, Mary answered, "Oh, I don't know. Maybe to smoke. I was just trying to help you retrace your steps. I'd really like a better look at Jayne's handiwork. I just didn't want to keep it."

"Oh." Sandra swallowed. "No, I don't smoke at work." She reached for her teacup and took a sip, but she seemed to be breathing quickly and shallowly.

Mary leaned forward to touch the woman on the knee. "Sandra, are you all right? You're a bit pale."

"I just..." Sandra reached for her purse, which was sitting on the coffee table, and rummaged around in it. She unearthed an asthma inhaler and took a quick breath from it.

She had asthma? Surely she wouldn't be smoking. Mary realized the windows must be open to air out the cigarette smoke.

Was there indeed someone staying with Sandra who smoked cigarettes? It would explain the duffel bag too. But why had Sandra said no one was staying with her?

Sandra really wasn't looking very well, so Mary rose to her feet. "I'm sorry you're not feeling well. I should let you get some rest. Here, let me take the tray for you." Mary set the cups back on the tray and carried it into the kitchen.

"Thank you." Sandra followed her. "You can just set it on the counter."

Mary set the tray on the counter next to the fridge and stole a glance at the pictures posted there. One was a child's photo from Mercy's Children, an international organization that paired donors with needy children from around the world. On the bottom of the photo was printed the child's name and where she was from: Pamela from Bolivia. Pamela had a wide, toothy grin and pigtails that stuck out from her head slightly, and her dark eyes shone at the camera as the photo was taken.

Another photo was of a group of teenage girls dressed in volleyball uniforms. They were gathered around Sandra, who was dressed in a sporty polo shirt and capris with sneakers, with a whistle on a cord around her neck. Sandra had her arms around the girls, and they all grinned at the camera. Mary guessed this was Sandra's volleyball team. She recognized three of them as the girls who had been chatting so comfortably with Sandra at the bank before the reenactment. There were a few other action shots of the girls playing in a game—one of a tall girl spiking the ball, another of a girl setting the ball, several others of the girls passing the ball.

There was also a photo of Sandra with a group of twenty-somethings, all of them in more formal attire as if they'd gone to a fancy party or perhaps a Broadway show. They were outside, at night, and it looked like they were in front of a well-known concert theater in Boston. Sandra looked happy to be with her friends as they all smiled into the camera. Mary didn't recognize any of them except Sophie Mershon, the owner of the Tea Shoppe. She hadn't realized Sandra and Sophie were friends, but then again, they both worked all day and wouldn't exactly be shopping together in downtown Ivy Bay on an afternoon.

What was curious was that there were no other photos on the fridge of friends, and no photos of family members. Just the picture of Pamela, the photos of Sandra's volleyball team, and the one group photo with Sandra's friends.

Mary bid Sandra good-bye, and the young woman might have looked relieved that Mary was going, but Mary couldn't quite tell because she still looked weak and tired from the coughing. Despite her feeling that something was off in the situation, Mary couldn't help but give Sandra a parting squeeze good-bye. "I hope you're feeling better soon. If this lingers much longer, it may not be something in the air, and you might want to see a doctor."

She'd feel terrible if there was something wrong with the poor girl and she'd misread the whole situation.

Still, as Mary drove home, she reflected that overall she was left with a feeling of... suspicion. It looked like someone was staying with Sandra. She remembered the low voice she'd heard before she knocked. Did Sandra and that other person have something to do with the robbery?

ELEVEN

---◆◆---

When Mary walked in the door, the warm smell of chicken soup made her mouth water. Gus greeted her by weaving through her ankles, and she guessed he was hungry too. She entered the kitchen to see Betty ladling the soup into a bowl.

"You're just eating now?" Mary asked.

"I dozed a little on the couch," Betty confessed, stifling a small yawn. "You have good timing. I'll make you a sandwich too, while you wash up."

After Mary had fed Gus and then washed her hands, she sat at their kitchen table with Betty, and her sister said grace for them. Then Mary dug into her chicken vegetable soup and turkey sandwich. She hadn't realized how hungry she was until she started eating.

"How was your day?" Mary asked. "You met with Eleanor, right?"

"Yes, we went over how Living History Day went. There were a few emergencies I hadn't known about that Eleanor handled, and vice versa, so we both think it was good that both of us were at different places in downtown."

"What kinds of emergencies?"

"Oh, like the goats."

Mary stared at Betty, amused. "Goats?"

"You didn't see them? Two goats escaped their exhibit and were prancing down Meeting House Road. They stole one tourist's bag of popcorn."

Mary burst into laughter. "No, I didn't know about that."

Betty looked exasperated, but then a smile quirked on her lips. "I suppose that is rather funny now. But at the time, all I could think about was to get those goats penned up before they bit someone."

"What else?" Mary asked. "Now I'm thinking I missed all the fun of Living History Day."

Betty gave her a mock stern glance. "It wasn't fun for me and Eleanor, believe me. That was probably the most exciting emergency. There were a few demonstrations that ran out of supplies, and we had to send someone to get more. Next year, we could use more people to act as gophers and guides. Even though the flyer had a map, I kept answering questions about where certain demonstrations were."

"I thought it looked great to have so many people in costume," Mary said. "I felt almost underdressed."

"Next year, why don't you go in costume?" Betty's face had a scheming look that Mary remembered from her childhood.

"If I do, I'll pick my own costume."

"Don't you trust me?"

"Nope."

The two sisters laughed together.

"How was your day?" Betty asked.

Mary realized there was a lot to catch Betty up on. Mary told Betty about Megan fixing her computer, and how Megan had had a falling-out with her computer club and was having a hard time at school. She also mentioned that she thought having Megan help her gave her a little more confidence in herself.

She then told Betty about the video someone had taken of the reenactment that made Mary believe the robber wasn't Steve, and since there wasn't enough evidence for the police to investigate, she was doing her own investigating.

Mary also told Betty about her reluctant suspicions about Jerry, Sandra, and especially Jayne. Betty was shocked, but listened to Mary's reasons for what she suspected about each of them.

"Could I see the listing for the clock?" Betty said.

"I was hoping you would. I'd love if you can tell me why she's selling it for less than what she bought it for."

"I can try."

They had already finished eating, but they left their dishes at the table and went to the living room. Mary set up her computer on the low table, and they sat together on the blue-and-white-striped damask sofa so they could see the screen. Mary brought up her e-mail and opened the link Megan had sent to her for the clock listing.

"Oh, I saw that clock in Jayne's store," Betty said immediately.

"You're sure the clock in this listing is the same clock in Gems and Antiques?" Mary asked. "I thought so, but I'm also not an antique expert."

"It's definitely the same clock. I kept thinking I wanted to get a better look at it, but when I was in Jayne's store earlier, I had only a minute to talk to Jayne about Living History

Day. I promised myself I'd get into the store later this week to check the clock out." Betty peered closer at the listing. "Oh my. It's a Pierre-Louis Paquet."

Mary had noticed that name on the online auction listing. "Who is that?"

"He was a French clockmaker who was quite famous at about the turn of the century. His clocks are very rare now and high in demand. How much did Jayne say she paid for this?"

Mary told her. "Jayne seemed to think she got a good deal."

"*Hmm.* A true fan of Paquet's work would certainly pay twice that for the clock."

"So why is she selling it on this Web site for less than what she paid for it? Are you sure it's a Paquet?"

"Yes. Jayne clearly says so here on the page."

"Jayne wouldn't be mistaken about the value of the clock, would she?"

Betty sent her an unbelieving stare. "Jayne Tucker? Not likely."

"This is getting stranger and stranger. First, Jayne lists this clock under a different name. Then she's selling it for less than what she paid for it when it's obviously much more valuable."

Betty scrolled through the photos of the clock on the Web site page. She reached the end and hesitated. "Is that it?"

"What do you mean?"

"Are those all the photos she has of it?"

"You know the person who called her—the phone number she tried to hide from me—said something similar."

"I'm not surprised. Jayne has taken a lot of photos, but she's missing a few angles."

Mary peered at the pictures. "To me, it seems like she got all the angles."

"It's not very easy to spot, but there are some parts of the clock that aren't shown because the photo angles don't overlap."

Mary frowned. "Are they important angles? I mean, it looks like she's missing only a corner of the top back and a small section of the side panel, and other places that aren't very important. She has lots of shots of the clockface and the interior mechanism."

"Yes, that's true. It's not as if people really need to see the entire side panel if it's all one piece of wood."

"She wouldn't be hiding something by not showing those angles, would she?" Mary said in a low voice. She didn't even want to think about the possibility of Jayne Tucker being dishonest like that. It just wasn't like her.

"Jayne?" Betty said in an incredulous voice. "No, I couldn't possibly believe she'd do that."

"To be honest, me neither."

They stared at the photos for a moment longer. Then Betty got to her feet. "Let's clean up the dishes. I think I'd like to turn in early tonight."

After the dinner dishes were cleaned, Betty headed out of the kitchen, grimacing as she moved.

"Do you want me to get you a heating pad?" Mary asked.

"No, it's not too bad. Oh, but I didn't pick up my pain medication at the pharmacy today. I knew I was forgetting something."

"Do you need it right away?"

"Not tonight. I'll pick it up tomorr—No, I can't go tomorrow. I have to stay home in the morning because a repairman is coming to look at that leak in the washing machine."

"Why don't I pick it up for you before I open up the store? The pharmacy opens early."

"You're sure? Thanks." Betty said good night and headed to her bedroom.

Mary sat at the kitchen table and stared into space. What a day she'd had. The strangest part had been her visit to Sandra tonight. She hadn't expected to do more than find out about the linen rope, but she'd discovered other more mysterious things.

What if Sandra was working with Steve? He might have escaped with the loot on his boat, and he was waiting for Sandra to join him. Or maybe he double-crossed her, took all the loot, and left her.

But Mary knew Steve better than Sandra, and she had a hard time believing he'd do that. But if Sandra was working with someone else who robbed the bank, then where was Steve?

Maybe Steve found out about the robbery and whoever Sandra was working with threatened him, so Steve escaped on his boat?

Mary laughed to herself. She couldn't believe she was dreaming up ways for her community members to do dastardly things. Next, she was going to say Eleanor was the one who dressed up as the robber.

Mary wondered if she was so suspicious because she didn't know that much about Sandra. She had learned more tonight than in the entire time she'd known her. Based on the photos on her fridge, Sandra supported a little girl in Bolivia through Mercy's Children, she coached a teenage girls' volleyball team, and she went out to a Boston theater with a group of people. And it looked like she and Sophie Mershon might be friends.

When talking to her tonight, Mary thought that Sandra seemed genuinely concerned about Steve, and she seemed like a good person. Mary didn't think even the bank closing would make her desperate enough to do something out of character like rob the bank she worked at.

Right now, she'd do that research on the clock.

Mary brought up her e-mail and reopened the link Megan had sent to her for the clock listing.

She studied the pictures. The clock looked the same as the one in the shop because of the painted design around the clockface. She thought she remembered seeing the same narrow scratch in the paint when she studied the clock earlier that day.

Mary also looked for some other Paquet pieces being sold online to compare to Jayne's, and the prices were astronomical. Jayne had gotten a very good deal on what she paid for the clock, because other Paquet clocks were going for almost twice that amount.

Maybe Jayne's clock wasn't as old as these other, more expensive clocks? Mary looked, but no, Jayne's clock was about the same age, or within a couple of years of the other clocks.

Jayne clearly said it was a genuine Paquet clock there on the online listing. Why was she selling the clock for less than what she paid for it? Mary didn't believe for a second that Jayne would be mistaken about the value of the clock.

Was Jayne hiding something by not showing the missing angles of the clock? Was it deliberate or an accident? The sections missing were small, so it couldn't have been a large stain or crack or anything like that.

Mary sat back against the couch. Tomorrow, she had to go back to Jayne's shop and take a look at that clock. She could bring her camera and perhaps sneak a few pictures of the angles missing from the online listing. She pulled up the listing again and double-checked which angles she would need to photograph. Most of the angles would be easy to take photos of, but one missing angle was the bottom back, right near the foot. It was a heavy clock, and she'd need to figure out how to move it away from the wall so she could see the bottom back. Well, she'd think of something.

She didn't want to think Jayne or Sandra had anything to do with the robbery, but there were some odd clues that seemed suspicious—the evidence someone was staying at Sandra's house and the secret clock listing being sold for less than its true value by a woman who was still missing funds at the bank. Unless she got to the bottom of all this, she wouldn't know if what they were hiding was related to the robbery or was about something else entirely.

The next morning, Mary got up bright and early in order to get the prescription from Betty and head to the pharmacy. Betty offered to have a pancake breakfast ready by the time Mary got back with the pain medication.

The pharmacy was surprisingly busy that early in the morning. There was already a small line of people dropping off prescriptions, so Mary scooted up to the end of the line.

She then realized that Sandra was standing in front of her. Mary wondered if she'd be able to engage Sandra in conversation or if Sandra's apparent nervousness at her questions last night would still linger.

"Hello, Sandra," she said.

Sandra turned around at the sound of Mary's voice, but the smile she gave was short and tight. "Hi, Mary." She then turned back around, but Mary could see that her shoulders were stiff.

Why was Sandra so tense? Had Mary touched too close to a truth Sandra wanted to hide last night, and that was why she was awkward with Mary today, or was it something else this morning?

Mary didn't want to push herself forward when Sandra obviously didn't want to talk to her, but the motherly side of her hoped Sandra was all right.

Finally, Sandra got to the front of the line and handed the pharmacist Jacob Ames her prescription. He nodded and told her it would be a few minutes, which Sandra probably already knew since other people ahead of her had handed in their prescriptions and were waiting patiently for them to be filled.

As Sandra turned away from the pharmacist's desk, she came face-to-face with Mary, and her eyes looked away from her.

But then Sandra abruptly gasped and dropped her purse.

The action was so unexpected that Mary was too surprised to move at first. Then she gathered her wits about her and bent down to help Sandra collect the items from her purse that had scattered across the smooth linoleum floor.

Mary wasn't paying particular attention to what she picked up, but then she grabbed two pieces of paper that had drifted out of the purse, and her eyes caught on the title of the first one: "Application for a U.S. Passport."

The second sheet of the application was half-hidden by the top sheet, but she could see part of section nineteen, "Travel Plans," and under "Date of Trip," Sandra had filled out a date that was three weeks from today.

Mary had barely picked up the papers when Sandra snatched them out of her hands, stuffing the application into her purse. She shoved the last few things on the floor back into her bag and then quickly straightened.

It had all happened in a few seconds, but Jacob Ames was glowering at them. "You going to give me your prescription, or are you going to make me wait longer?" he said to Mary.

Sandra suddenly turned back to him and said, "Mr. Ames, I'll pick my prescription up later this afternoon."

"Be sure you come back before closing," he told her curtly, then held his hand out to Mary. "Well?"

Mary hastily gave him Betty's prescription, but she turned to watch as Sandra skirted the last few people in the line and hurried out of the pharmacy.

"It'll be a while," Jacob told Mary. "Have a seat." He jabbed his chin at a few plastic chairs in a small waiting area to the right of the prescription drop-off counter.

Mary walked away from the counter in a daze. What had just happened? What had caused Sandra to drop her purse like that? She'd looked at Mary first, and then she'd seen something....

Mary turned to nonchalantly see who was in the pharmacy—who would have been in Sandra's line of sight. There were two people in line behind Mary—a young mother with a three-year-old boy running a truck around on the ground at her feet, who was now handing her prescription to the pharmacist, and a teenage boy with his baseball cap on backward, who was texting someone on his cell phone or playing a game or something like that.

In the aisles behind Mary, an elderly woman with a pinched face squinted at the back of a bottle of vitamins, while a woman with tattoos and a leather biker jacket was picking out a tube of toothpaste, and a dark-haired, squat man looked back and forth between the two boxes of Band-Aids in his hands.

Mary had heard a man's voice at Sandra's house last night; perhaps this was him. She studied the man. He looked a bit dangerous. How would Sandra know him? At the same time, there was something about his face that made Mary think she might have even seen him before, but she couldn't place him.

The man looked up and caught her staring. He raised his eyebrows at her as if to ask what she was doing, then went back to looking at his boxes of Band-Aids.

Mary's thoughts went back to Sandra. What had startled her? Was it this surly-looking man? And why had she been applying for a passport? Where was Sandra going, and why was she leaving?

And, as much as Mary knew it was none of her business, she couldn't help but wonder: Where had Sandra gotten the money to travel internationally?

It always came back to money: Money was what Jerry had mentioned in his argument with Steve; Jayne's money was missing from the bank. And now here was Sandra, about to leave the country in three weeks' time, when her job was potentially on the line. Was Sandra trying to escape? Surely not.

But then again . . .

Sandra obviously hadn't been the masked robber, but was Sandra somehow involved with an accomplice—perhaps with Steve, as Mary had already wondered—and now she was trying to escape with what they'd stolen? Or instead of Steve, was she working with whoever had been smoking those cigarettes at her house? Or, Mary could barely allow the thought: Could it really be Jayne?

Yet if Sandra was working with someone else, then where was Steve? Why was he missing? Was he all right? She prayed once again that he was all right. Perhaps he'd found out about Sandra's plans and was somehow in danger, and so he escaped on his boat. But surely he would realize it would make him look guilty.

Mary told herself to calm her buzzing thoughts and think carefully. Yes, the passport application was suspicious, but it didn't directly tie Sandra to the robbery.

Mary had to get to the bottom of this, for Steve's sake. She just hoped that there was a reasonable explanation when she got there, and that she could figure it out in time.

TWELVE

W hen Mary returned home with Betty's prescription, she arrived just in time to hear Betty say, "Oh, wait, Rebecca. Mary just walked in. Mary! Rebecca's on the phone."

Mary picked up the receiver. "Hello?"

"Hi, Mary. I'm sorry, but I can't come into work this morning. Ashley has a really bad toothache. It looks like she chipped a tooth. I managed to get an appointment with the dentist this morning. I hope it won't take too long and I can be at work by lunchtime."

"Oh, poor Ashley!"

"Yeah, she's in a lot of pain."

"Well, don't worry about work. I hope Ashley feels better soon." Mary's tooth ached in sympathy for Ashley. She didn't like going to the dentist all that much.

As she said good-bye and hung up, Betty turned from the stove where she was flipping pancakes. "Ashley needs to go to the dentist?"

"Yes, she has a toothache."

Betty winced. "Ouch."

"That's what I was thinking when she told me."

"You and I both never cared for the dentist, did we?" Betty brought the plate of pancakes to the kitchen.

"What I hated most was the smell of the dentist's office." Mary set the table with plates and utensils.

"Yes, exactly."

"And there was the sound of the whirring of the drill." Mary shuddered. "Although to be honest, I think it was actually just the whirring of the circular tooth polisher he used to clean our teeth."

"It still sounded awful." Betty set the maple syrup on the table and sat down.

They said grace and dug in. "Great pancakes, Bets," Mary said.

"It's all in the butter. I used lots of it."

"This is a nice treat. We don't often do this in the middle of the week."

"I figured you deserved a reward for getting up early to get my prescription filled."

Mary grinned. "I refuse to jump out of an airplane, swim in shark-infested waters, or run a marathon for you, but I'm willing to do anything else."

"So there are limits to your love for me? Don't tell me you're afraid of itty-bitty sharks."

"I actually think I'm more afraid of spiders than sharks, so add spider-filled attics to that list."

"Check."

They both laughed, and then a comfortable silence fell between them. Mary loved the camaraderie she'd always shared with her sister, and she especially loved their closeness now that they lived together. They'd had their own lives for so long, but now, living with Betty, Mary was reminded of the close bond they'd had as young girls, a bond that was strengthening here in Ivy Bay.

"What are your plans for today?" Mary asked.

"Betsy and Allison are out of school this week because of fall break, so I'm going to pick them up and take them to the beach," Betty said.

Mary sighed. "You're so lucky. I wish my grandchildren lived closer to me."

"Believe me, I know how lucky I am. Are you doing anything special besides minding the shop?"

"No. I might go across the street to Jayne's store to see how she's doing." And possibly take a look at that clock that was-and-yet-wasn't for sale.

Mary and Betty finished breakfast. Then Betty said she'd wash up so Mary could get to work. She put Gus in his carrier and headed to the store.

It ended up being a busy morning. She had several people come in who were all part of a craft group that met once a month, and at the meeting last night, they'd been discussing a recent series of cozy mystery books. Several of them came in to buy copies, and luckily, Mary had several copies of each book in the series in stock, although she had to go into the back to search through some boxes for the extra copies she hadn't put out on the shelves.

While she was there searching, she came across a box of damaged books. Some had been returned by customers, while others had gotten a bit worn from people handling them in the store. They were still in great reading shape, just not in any shape to be resold.

Mary made a mental note to give the books away. She often had damaged books to give away, and maybe this time, she could give the books to a different charity organization. She remembered her interactions with Megan the past few days, and she also remembered the junior high school girls Sandra worked with on her volleyball team. Maybe she'd talk to her neighbor Sherry Walinski about a school library she could donate the books to.

In the lull in between customers, Mary took time to look up the cigarettes she'd seen at Sandra's house: Veryan Chapp kretek cigarettes. They were apparently made in India and were a type of clove cigarette, which explained why they didn't smell like normal cigarettes. They had a very strong flavor, slightly sweet, which matched the scent she remembered. They weren't terribly rare or unusual—this brand was apparently widely distributed on the East Coast, especially in Boston—but they weren't as common as the cigarettes she always saw the fishermen smoking at the docks.

She was so engrossed in reading about the cigarettes that she was slow to look up when the chime over the front door rang. "Welcome, may I help you?" The last word came out a little like a croak because the customer who had just come into her store was the same seedy-looking man she had seen talking to Jayne yesterday.

It was definitely him. He wore different clothes than he had before, but they were still in plain gray and brown colors, making him almost blend into the woodwork. His long, narrow face had a hint of slyness and cunning, and Mary instinctively drew back slightly when she saw him.

No, what was she doing? She had to talk to him and try to find out what he was talking to Jayne about.

She reinserted the smile on her face and asked, "Is there anything I can help you with?"

He hadn't noticed her initial start of surprise at seeing him, because he'd been looking around the shop and not at her. Now he turned toward her and asked, "Got any maps of the area?"

She didn't at the moment, but she wanted to keep him here longer. "What kind of map do you need? I mean, how detailed and what types of landmarks do you want it to show?"

"Street map." His words were clipped and impatient.

"Of just Ivy Bay or the surrounding area?"

"Surrounding."

A man of few words. Mary pretended to look through the cubbyholes behind the counter as she asked conversationally, "Are you from far away?"

"Argyle," he said.

The town sounded familiar to Mary, but she couldn't immediately place it in her memory. However, she made a mental note to remember it so she could look it up later. "Is that very far from Ivy Bay?"

"A couple of hours," he said curtly, clearly not in the mood to talk.

She didn't want to interrogate him, but she did want to find out what his name was. "Well, welcome to Ivy Bay. I'm Mary Fisher." She thrust a hand toward the man with a bright smile.

"I'm"—he seemed startled at first, then shook her hand— "Greig Davies."

"Greeg? That's an unusual name."

"G-R-E-I-G. It's Scottish." He went on with a touch of impatience, "Do you have the map I need?"

Mary couldn't stall any longer. "Oh, I'm sorry. I don't think so. But I think the souvenir store just down the street might have what you're looking for."

"Thanks," he grunted, and escaped from her shop before she could say anything more.

Mary immediately went to her computer and looked up Greig Davies and the town he had mentioned, and the first Web site that popped up was for Greig Davies, private investigator.

Why would Jayne be talking to a private investigator? She'd also spoken to him outside instead of in her shop. Did she not want people to see her speaking to him? Mary wondered if the secretive air of the meeting meant that Jayne's husband, Rich, didn't know about this man. Did this have to do with Jayne's missing money? Steve's disappearance? The clock?

Greig's Web site listed a toll-free voice-mail phone number, so she called to leave a message.

"This is Greig Davies, private investigator. Please leave a message."

A very no-nonsense voice-mail greeting. Mary cleared her throat. "Hello, my name is Mary. I would love to talk to you when you have time. Please call me." She gave her cell phone number rather than the shop number just in case he called and Rebecca picked up the phone.

Bob Hiller came into the shop with his mailbag. "Morning, Mary. Got a few things for you."

Mary always had her books shipped with a shipping company rather than through the postal mail, so she knew he wouldn't have more than letters, bills, and advertisements. "How are you doing, Bob?"

"Ah well, my knee is acting up a bit, but that might be because a dog ran into me yesterday."

"Goodness, are you all right?"

"Oh, Spotty was just excited to come say hi to me, and since he's a growing puppy, he doesn't know his own strength. Knocked his big head right into my kneecap. It'll be fine in a day or so."

Bob handed over the electric bill for the store and a manila envelope with the return address of Gibson Overfield, the boat broker whose secretary had spoken with Mary yesterday over the phone. This must be the packet of information she'd promised. Mary was surprised that the secretary had sent the envelope through overnight express mail since it was extra expense, but then again, Boston wasn't very far away, and it was obvious Gibson Overfield was very successful. He probably garnered more sales by striking while the iron was hot, rather than allowing for a few days to pass by, during which a customer might not be as interested in buying a boat as they were before.

"Buying a boat?" Bob joked.

"No, but I did meet this boat broker yesterday at the docks."

"He must have been a good salesman to get you to accept a sales packet."

"Yes, I had a hard time saying no."

Bob nodded as he headed out of the store. "See you later."

"Bye, Bob. Thanks."

Mary opened her mail and then opened the packet of information from Gibson Overfield's secretary. The first sheet was a nicely printed letter thanking her for calling yesterday and including contact information if she was interested in any of the boats in the packet. The rest of the envelope included several glossy sheets of boats for sale, with lots of full-color photographs and the features of the boats. The boats for sale ranged from inexpensive small boats to large yachts even bigger than the one she'd seen Jerry on.

She searched for the boat she'd seen, but couldn't find it among the sheets in the packet. Had he already bought the boat, and was that why it wasn't in the packet? She spread the sheets out on the countertop to look at them better.

The door chimed again, and Henry walked in. "Good morning."

"Good morning. Are you just back from fishing?"

"Yep. Had a good run this morning." His eyes fell on the sheets with the pictures of boats. "Are you buying a boat?"

She laughed. "No, this is just a packet a boat broker sent to me."

Being a fisherman, Henry couldn't seem to resist sorting through the pages. Then he uncovered one page that made him stop. "Is this—?" He peered more closely at one boat.

"What is it?" Mary asked.

"I didn't know Jerry was selling his boat."

The boat Henry pointed out wasn't the expensive yacht she'd seen Jerry and Gibson Overfield on yesterday. This boat was entirely different—smaller, sleeker, good for fishing but not as luxurious as a pleasure boat. According to the boat specs, it was also relatively new.

"I didn't know that, but I suppose I shouldn't be surprised he owns a boat. Sometimes it seems everyone in Ivy Bay sails or owns a boat of their own since we're right on the water."

"You don't," Henry said with a wink. "I'm wondering if you requested this packet because subconsciously you want to catch up with all the rest of us who sail."

Mary rolled her eyes. "I'm so busy the last thing I need is a boat to take care of." A thought occurred to her. "The description says this boat is pretty new."

Henry ran his finger down the boat specs on the sheet. "It's only a couple of years old. Jerry must have bought it new, but he kept it only a short time."

"But I'm confused. Why is he selling it if he just bought it?"

Henry frowned as he read the specs on the sheet. "Maybe he needs the money. He's selling it for below value."

The Avakians must need quite a bit of money, and quickly, if they were selling this boat below value. Yesterday, Jerry must have been speaking to Gibson Overfield because he'd commissioned him to sell his own boat, not because Jerry wanted to buy a boat.

What did all this have to do with Jerry's argument with Steve behind the bank just before the robbery? He'd accused Steve of being stubborn about "the money." Now suspecting that Jerry was in need of money, Mary wondered if Jerry was indeed involved in the robbery somehow. Would he do something like that if he was in desperate need? He might have collaborated with Steve, or he might have robbed the bank himself—he was the right height to pose as the robber. If Steve wasn't involved, where was he? Did Jerry do something to him, or perhaps had Steve found out what Jerry was going to do and ran away to protect himself?

Henry gave her a wary look. "I know that expression on your face, Mary, and I can guess where your thoughts are going. But I know Jerry wouldn't do anything like rob a bank, no matter how desperate he might be."

Mary gave a little laugh. "You're right. It seems terrible to be suspecting our community members of doing something so awful. But that's the main reason I don't think Steve is guilty of it, and yet he's the only suspect the police are pursuing. I can't sit and do nothing when I think the police are wrong. I need to pursue every clue."

"I can understand that. I don't think Steve did it either. I just don't know who would."

"It doesn't help that Steve and his boat are gone. It only makes him look more guilty, but I can't help thinking that's what the true robber wants the police to think."

"Speaking of Steve's boat, today I had a chat with a friend of mine who works for the coast guard. He mentioned that they've been on the lookout for Steve's boat, and they even stopped one or two that looked like his boat, but they haven't found it."

"Maybe whoever took the boat gave the coast guard the slip?"

"It's possible, but they were alerted within an hour of the robbery."

"Maybe Steve hid the boat before the robbery."

"If that's the case, then there's a good chance it's still in the area. Once the robber tries to sail the boat away, the coast guard will catch him."

The store phone rang, and Henry said good-bye so she could answer it. It was Bernice Foster, a member of Mary's prayer group, who wanted Mary to order the first book in a new mystery series for her.

The morning went quickly after that because she had a steady stream of customers and phone calls. However, just before lunchtime, Mary happened to look out the front window at Jayne's store and caught her putting out a Be Back in One Hour sign in the door.

Well, Mary supposed her visit to Jayne's store at lunchtime was out. She'd have to go later this afternoon.

Rebecca arrived with Ashley, whose right cheek was puffy.

"How are you feeling?" Mary asked the girl.

"Oh-kay." Her speech was muffled.

"Was it a chipped tooth?" Mary asked Ashley's mother.

"Yep. The dentist was able to repair it, but it was so sensitive and she kept flinching in the chair that he ended up numbing her entire right side. So for today, she's my lopsided chipmunk." Rebecca grinned and gave Ashley an affectionate pinch of her oversized cheek.

Ashley rolled her eyes and managed to look like she was a disgruntled thirteen-year-old rather than a seven-year-old. *"Mommm…"*

"At least it doesn't hurt now," Mary said. "And I bet you had a great lunch."

Ashley grinned, which looked endearing with her puffy cheek. "Ice cream."

The store phone rang, and Mary answered. "Hello. Mary's Mystery Bookshop."

"Hi, Mary. This is Victoria Pickerton."

"Hi, Victoria. Don't tell me you've already got a new copy of that book in?"

"Even better. I found the missing one. I figured it was misshelved, and when I looked at the cover online, I had a hunch that one of my library assistants might have mistaken it for a fiction book, so I looked in the adult-fiction section, and there it was. The sticker on the spine had gotten partially rubbed off, so whoever shelved it didn't even notice it was supposed to be in nonfiction."

"That's wonderful, Victoria. Can I come pick it up right now?"

"I'll be waiting."

After Mary hung up the phone, she noticed that Rebecca had already put her things away. "Go ahead. I'll watch the shop. And get yourself some lunch while you're at it."

Mary smiled. "Yes, Mom."

Rebecca winked at her.

It took only a few minutes for her to walk to the library and pick up the book. She immediately sat down at a table and found the chapter on the Ivy Bay Bank & Trust robbery.

The book had been written during the last days of Elias Cowper's life, when he was waiting to be hanged for his crimes, and he had confessed all to the biographer—or rather, he had confessed all that he'd wanted to confess. He'd been deliberately vague at several points, whether to protect his associates or from a hope he'd escape and utilize some of his old hiding places and old tricks.

She was a bit disappointed that the Ivy Bay robbery itself was rather straightforward. Elias Cowper had shot the bank manager in the leg, but witnesses say it looked like the gun simply misfired rather than that Elias was aiming for the man. He'd taken two bags of money from the vault—then, it had been the main vault, while today, it was the safe-deposit vault—and escaped.

What was curious was that the sheriff didn't find Elias because he'd found, in Elias's own words, "a hovel guarded by an oak tree with a root cellar," which apparently no one knew about. The biographer had clarified in a footnote that it had been a fisherman's shanty by the Ivy Bay docks. He'd hidden there for a few days and then snuck away in the dead of night while the sheriff was out combing the countryside for him.

Mary wondered if that fisherman's shanty was still there. Could it really be that simple and Steve had hidden out there like Elias Cowper had done? It seemed incredible—and incredibly simplistic—but she didn't have many other clues as to where Steve might be, and this book was the closest she'd gotten to understanding what might have been going through Steve's head.

The fact that the book was missing was also a clue. If the book wasn't important, why was it suddenly gone? Steve or whoever the robber had been had no reason to take the book with him unless the book was significant for some reason.

Maybe the robber used some of the aspects of the original robbery, thinking they'd serve him as well as they'd served Elias Cowper since the original robbery was so old and not well known in Ivy Bay. There were old property records at the clerk's office, which housed the old city archives. Would one of the property records show the shanty?

Mary headed back to Main Street but felt her stomach growling, so she stopped in the Tea Shoppe. As soon as she entered, the smell of bacon and cheese made her mouth water. She glanced at the teapot-shaped chalkboard and saw that Sophie's delicious bacon, spinach, and cheddar cheese quiche was the special for today. With the luscious smell filling the busy shop, Mary couldn't resist deciding to get the quiche.

She moved to get in line to order, and at the end of the line, she spied the man from Neels Banking Group. He looked a bit like a judge as he frowned intently at a chicken-salad sandwich that he'd apparently gotten from the refrigerator.

"I hope your sandwich hasn't offended you," Mary said to him with a smile.

Startled, he looked up at her, but instead of relaxing, his frown deepened. "No. I was just thinking of something else."

Mary said in a cheerful voice, "If you have time, you should check out some of the local sights and restaurants. Sam's Seafood down by the marina is in one of the oldest buildings in town. There's nothing like eating fish and chips with the view of the marina and fishing fleet."

The man gave her a quick glance but didn't answer her.

Mary went on, "Or if you have a sweet tooth, Bailey's Ice Cream Shop down the street is a vintage ice-cream parlor, and all their ice creams are homemade. I make ice cream myself, and Tess Bailey features one of my flavors each month. This month, it's pumpkin with maple chips and graham-cracker crust."

The man gave a short exhale and turned to her with an icy stare. "I beg your pardon, but I would appreciate a bit of peace and quiet while I'm waiting in line."

The customer in front of him finished her order and walked away, and he moved up to the counter to pay for his sandwich.

Mary reflected with chagrin that she had been a bit chatty. Still, she hoped his bad mood wasn't because Ivy Bay Bank & Trust's financials were in bad shape. It would be so heartbreaking for the bank to close, especially considering the shock everyone seemed to be feeling following the scandalous robbery.

The man paid quickly, and then it was Mary's turn. "Hi, Sophie. I'd love a slice of that quiche to go."

"Sure, Mary." Sophie twirled to get the quiche from the table behind the counter, her long sunlight-colored braid swinging with her graceful movements.

As Sophie rang up her order, Mary remembered the photo she'd seen on Sandra's fridge. "I was at Sandra Rink's house yesterday and saw a photo of you with Sandra and a bunch of friends having a night out. You all looked so young and lively."

Sophie threw Mary a startled look. "A night out?"

"You all were dressed up and looked like you'd been to a play or concert in Boston."

"Oh, that's right. A couple of months ago, Sandra had an extra ticket for the ballet, and she invited me to join her and her other friends."

"That must have been fun. I suppose you two don't meet much during working hours."

"Actually, that was the first time I've been out with Sandra and her friends. The ballet was great." Sophie handed Mary her change. "Thanks, Mary. Have a good day."

Mary was a bit disappointed at the results of her lunchtime interactions. She hadn't discovered anything interesting about either the man from the Neels Banking Group or about Sandra. She'd struck out twice! Well, hopefully when Jayne reopened the store this afternoon, Mary would be able to get a good look at that clock. And then maybe she'd finally figure out what was at the bottom of Jayne's strange behavior.

THIRTEEN

Mary had just walked back into the store from lunch when the phone rang. Rebecca was helping another customer look for a book, so Mary answered the phone, but it kept ringing. She stared at the handset in confusion before realizing the ringing was from her cell phone. She hadn't even noticed the difference in ringtone. Chuckling to herself, she pulled her cell phone out and saw that it was Greig Davies, the private investigator. She eagerly answered it.

"Hello, this is Mary." She tried to alter her voice a bit, making it a little lower.

"This is Greig Davies. You called?"

He certainly didn't beat around the bush. "Yes, thank you for returning my call. I had a few questions for you."

"Yes?"

"I was wondering what type of investigating you did?"

"Anything you need me to do, lady."

Mary tried to think through what she knew. Jayne had been upset at the reenactment and had tried to hide the fact she was selling the clock for less than what she paid for it. "Do you ever investigate antiques? Trying to find certain pieces?"

"Antiques? No, I've never done that. Why, is that what you needed?"

"No, I was just curious."

"If you need someone to find an antique for you, I'd recommend you ask an antique dealer instead."

"I guess I thought you might do things like that because of an antique dealer who's one of your clients."

Greig gave a long sigh. "One thing about being a private investigator is that I keep my clients' information private. I'm afraid I can't speak about anyone or anything else I've been doing."

Mary supposed she should have known that.

Greig continued, "Did you want to hire me for a job?"

Mary couldn't lie. "Not exactly. I just wanted to know more about you."

"Like I said, I keep my clients' secrets, and I investigate anything you want me to. Did you need to know anything else about me?"

Mary thought a moment but couldn't think of anything she wanted to know from him that didn't involve him working for Jayne. "I suppose not."

"Well, if you need me, just give me a call. Good-bye." And he hung up.

Something occurred to Mary then, as her mind recalled the man in the Tea Shoppe. What if Jayne had hired the private investigator because of her missing deposit at the bank? What if Jayne's missing deposit wasn't a computer error, as the bank claimed? What if Steve and Sandra together, or maybe just one or the other of them, stole Jayne's money? That was why it was missing, and they were blaming it on some error at the bank. The rumor was that Jayne lost a lot of money. If it was a large enough amount, the accountant from the Neels Banking Group could be here to investigate it.

Steve could have robbed the bank as a distraction from the real theft of Jayne's money—the timing was certainly coincidental enough, the robbery happening right before the accountant was scheduled to arrive in Ivy Bay. She'd focused on what had been stolen from the safe-deposit boxes, but it could be that Jayne's missing funds were more than the amount stolen in the robbery. They needed to steal only enough from the safe-deposit boxes to present a distraction for the police. Or maybe they were greedy and the money from the robbery was in addition to what they took from Jayne, and now Steve or Sandra or both of them intended to leave town with their loot.

Both Steve and Sandra had seemed worried about losing their jobs at the bank in light of the rumors about Neels closing several other banks in the state. They'd have a motive for stealing Jayne's money and robbing the vault during the reenactment.

They both looked suspicious, but it was still hard to imagine either of them doing it. And if Sandra didn't rob the bank with Steve as an accomplice, who did she work with?

Rebecca and the customer she was helping moved toward the counter. Mary got out of the way so Rebecca could ring up the sale. As she looked out the front window of the store, she saw that Jayne's store was open again, but Jayne was just leaving, perhaps to run an errand.

As she grabbed her purse, she caught Rebecca's eye and made a hand motion that she'd be back soon. Then she headed across the street to Jayne's store. Mary's digital camera was still in her purse from Living History Day—she'd thought about removing it, but then left it in yesterday when she decided to take her own photos of the clock.

When Mary entered the shop, Rich came out from the back and smiled as he saw her. "Hi, Mary. How are you doing? How's the shop?"

"We weren't very busy after Living History Day, but now things are picking up. How're things with you?"

"It's been nonstop since Living History Day. Were you at the robbery reenactment?"

"Yes, I was in the bank. Were you?"

Rich shook his head. "I was minding the store. I can't believe something like that would happen in broad daylight. And from Steve."

"It was such a sad note for Living History Day. Otherwise, it was turning out to be quite a busy event."

Rich nodded. "For us, definitely." He gestured to the store. "We're actually down in inventory a bit, so if you're shopping, things are a little sparse right now. Did you need help finding something?"

Mary shook her head. "I'm just looking."

"Well, if you have any questions, just holler. I'll be right at the back of the store."

Then Rich left Mary to her own devices, which was exactly what she'd been hoping would happen. Rich often did work in the back room, and if Jayne wasn't minding the counter, he came out only when a customer entered the store.

Mary sidled through the store in search of the clock.

It was standing where she'd seen it before, and it still had the Not for Sale sign on it. Mary got out her camera and started taking pictures of the sections missing in the photos on the online listing.

Her heart sank when she saw that the clock was close to the wall. She'd have to find a way to nudge it askew so she could take a picture of the back side near the leg, one of the missing photo angles. Fortunately, Jayne had put furniture coasters under the four feet. Mary hadn't remembered seeing that when she looked at the clock before. The coasters were made to allow heavy furniture to be easily moved around and were meant to protect the floor from furniture legs causing scratches, but the coasters would also allow Mary to easily slide the clock away from the wall.

Mary gingerly tested how heavy it was. It was heavy, but not as much as she feared. The clock was only about five feet tall and very narrow, and it had elegantly carved claw feet at the bottom rather than a square base resting directly on the floor.

Mary got a firm grip on the sides of the clock. She gave a gentle push and slid it so that it angled away from the wall. She didn't want to break the clock, so she was very careful as she handled it. The coasters on the four feet made a slight *shushing* noise, and the clock moved almost as if on wheels.

Mary bent to look at the back of the clock. On the back panel, in the missing photo angle, was a small dark spot. Mary took out her camera and tried to take a picture.

Unfortunately, the area near the floor was too far away from the store windows and overhead lights and was too dark. Any picture she tried to take without the flash was barely visible, but Mary worried that using the flash might get Rich's attention.

She peered toward the back of the store and saw that Rich had disappeared into the back room. He definitely wouldn't see if she used her camera flash.

Mary took several photos of the back bottom leg of the clock, just for good measure.

She was just in time, because as she stowed her camera away and gently pushed the clock back in place against the wall, she heard Jayne's voice as she reentered the shop.

"Rich, did you get a chance to examine that brooch? I just met someone who might be interested." She stopped when she saw Mary emerge from behind some antique dressers. "Oh, hi, Mary. I didn't know you were in here."

"I stopped in on the spur of the moment," Mary said. "I was only browsing." Something that Jayne had said as she walked in triggered a quiet note of recognition in her brain. "What brooch were you talking about as you walked in?"

"This one." Jayne was always eager to tell people about the lovely antiques she unearthed, and now was no different. She moved to the glass-covered front counter and took out a brooch with a dark-red stone. "It's Italian," Jayne said. "I think it's from the early eighteenth century. Rich was going to examine the stone to see if it was garnet or something else."

Mary admired the delicate gold wirework. "This is new, isn't it?"

"Yes, I got it last week at an estate sale, but I hadn't yet dated it until yesterday, so we didn't put it out until today."

Mary could see they hadn't yet put on a sales price either. "I remember you mentioning you had a good haul last week." Mary grinned at Jayne. "Was this from that estate sale?"

Jayne nodded. "It was from one of three estate sales we went to last weekend. I found things at most of them."

Had Jayne laid a slight stress on the word *most*, or was that Mary's imagination? Mary suddenly put two and two together. But she'd still need to check the photos of the clock first.

"The brooch is beautiful," Mary said. "Do you know yet what the price will be?"

"Not until Rich examines the gemstone. You might have to wait in line, though, because I just ran into Marnie Reid on the street and she asked if I had any antique brooches with red stones. She wants it to match a dress she just bought."

Mary smiled. "Marnie has such lovely, romantic tastes. I think she'll love this."

At that moment, a customer came into the shop, so Mary said, "I'll let you get back to work. See you later, Jayne."

"See you, Mary."

Mary went back across the street to her store. She entered the shop, where Rebecca was chatting with another customer at one of the shelves. Mary went to the computer and hooked up her camera to download the photos.

While the photos were transferring, she did a quick search online for a map of Swansea, a town about an hour away from Ivy Bay.

Right next to Swansea was Argyle. She had a feeling that the reason Jayne hired Greig was because of the estate sale in that part of the county.

The photos finished uploading, so she took a look at them. Most of the photos she'd taken without the flash were fine except for the ones of the bottom back leg of the clock. As she'd feared, the first few of those pictures were too dark to be able to see much. However, Mary peered at the shots anyway, which showed only an age spot on the wood.

Then she looked at the pictures she got with the flash. The spot still looked a great deal like an age spot, but there was a definite line here, a curve there, that looked more man-made. Mary zoomed in on her computer screen. She'd gotten the camera about a foot away from the clock, and she'd used her camera's autofocus function, so the resolution was rather good.

The age spot looked like...a logo.

Why wouldn't Jayne have shown the clockmaker's logo on the clock? Was it an accident that she didn't include this particular angle on the photos?

The logo looked like two intertwined letters, *B* and *S*, so Mary did an Internet search for clockmaker logos. It took her a while, but she finally found a photo of a logo for a watchmaker, Blythe-Stewart. The photo showed a clearer logo than the one on Jayne's clock, but it was definitely the same.

Which meant this was certainly not a Pierre-Louis Paquet clock.

How long had Blythe-Stewart been in business? Maybe the clock was an antique and really was worth what Jayne was selling it for, even if it was not a Paquet clock.

Mary found the watchmaker's Web site. She went to the About page to look at their history.

Blythe-Stewart was founded in 1943. They weren't even in business at the time this clock was supposed to have been made.

The clock must be a complete fake. The mechanisms looked old and very different from the Blythe-Stewart clocks Mary found online. Mary guessed that someone deliberately put old mechanisms in the Blythe-Stewart clock and then painted it and altered it to look like a Paquet. That was probably why Jayne thought it was a true Paquet, especially if the seller told her it was.

Now Mary knew why Jayne hadn't shown that angle in her photos of the clock. She had suspected something like this when she put everything together—reselling it online under a false name for lower than what she paid for it, the lack of certain photos on the online listing, and also the private investigator being from the same town as the estate sale where she bought it. Mary guessed that Jayne hired the private investigator to find the person who sold her the clock.

Mary bit her lip. What bothered her was that Jayne was still trying to sell it online as a Paquet clock. Was it a typo? If Jayne were to sell this as a Blythe-Stewart clock, how much would she sell it for? Mary did a quick Web search and easily found that a Blythe-Stewart clock would sell for only about half the amount on Jayne's online listing.

So Jayne was doing this deliberately. The proof of Jayne's dishonesty twisted inside Mary. This was so out of character for Jayne. She'd always been so scrupulous to give fair prices for her antiques and verify the provenance of a piece with as much detail as she could. Why would she suddenly do this?

Was she desperate for money? The bank still hadn't found her deposit.

No, if she'd been desperate for money and had indeed had something to do with the robbery, she wouldn't need to continue to sell this clock online. No one had bid on it yet, so she could easily take down the auction entry.

Mary realized that this was why Jayne had been acting strangely for the past few days—actually, for the past week or so. She didn't have anything to do with the robbery, Mary was sure. Instead, Jayne was probably feeling conflicted about selling a fake clock as a real Paquet antique.

Mary discovered her hands were trembling. She was sad, confused, and anxious about what she'd just discovered.

Should she go talk to Jayne about this? A part of Mary didn't want to say anything, but she knew that talking to Jayne would be the right thing to do. She didn't want to hurt Jayne, but she needed to speak to her about what she was doing.

Maybe Mary was wrong. Jayne would be upset at her for thinking she'd do something so underhanded.

Or maybe there was some misunderstanding and Jayne didn't realize what she was doing. She would want Mary to tell her, if that were the case.

What should she do?

———

Mary told Rebecca she'd be out again and then left the shop to head to the county clerk's office. Now that she knew about the fisherman's shanty that Elias Cowper used, she figured it was worth a shot to see if it was still in Ivy Bay. The fact the book was missing seemed to indicate something in it was significant to the robber, and so she wanted to explore the shanty in case that was something the robber had used.

As she exited the store, she saw the Avakians heading down Main Street. They turned into the Black & White Diner.

To be honest, Jerry intimidated her a little, partly because she'd seen him so upset when she interrupted his conversation with Steve behind the bank. She remembered how he had seemed very aggressive in his stance and his voice. She knew he was a nice man, but she wasn't close enough to him to understand his moods.

Mary wanted to be able to get Patricia on her own, without Jerry, in order to talk to her about the boat they were selling. Patricia had seemed anxious to hide the fact that they were selling the boat—although since Mary hadn't known they owned a boat, the book title had led her to believe they were buying a boat, not selling one. If for some reason she wanted to keep their actions regarding their boat secret, would she just avoid the topic when talking to Mary?

But Mary just couldn't get it out of her head that it seemed odd and coincidental for them to be selling their boat for below value just after Jerry had been having that intense conversation with Steve about money. Then the robbery happened, and Steve and his boat disappeared. Did the Avakians have anything to do with that? Was it at all possible that Jerry would do something like kidnap Steve and take his place in the reenactment in order to rob the bank? It could have been a spur-of-the-moment thing. And perhaps he hadn't gotten as much from those few safe-deposit boxes he'd stolen, and that's why he was trying to sell his boat, as well.

Even though it seemed unlikely Patricia would talk to her about the boat, Mary decided to try to speak one-on-one with Patricia. It had to be soon, especially if Jerry and Patricia knew what had happened to Steve.

Lord, I know I sound like a broken record, but I pray Steve is all right, she whispered, as she walked down the street.

The county clerk's office wasn't far from her bookstore. As soon as she entered the small building, she could smell the must from the old records that were stored in the cramped space.

Bea Winslow sat behind the counter and smiled at Mary as she walked in. "Hi, Mary. Welcome. Say, did Megan fix your computer?"

"Yes, she's amazing," Mary said.

"She has good genes." Bea winked at Mary. "I'm glad you needed her help this week, actually. She's been a little down lately, and it helps when she has something to do."

"I definitely needed her," Mary said. "I also sent her on a little Internet scavenger hunt. I thought it might keep her occupied longer than it did." Mary recalled how quickly Megan had found Jayne's Internet listing. "She's pretty bright."

"She must have liked that. She loves puzzles and things."

"Does she?"

"She hates not knowing the answer to something. Well," Bea corrected herself, "if it's something that interests her. She seems fine not knowing the answer to her history homework."

Bea and Mary grinned at each other.

"What other things does she like to do?" Mary asked.

Bea thought a moment. "She really enjoys helping people. She's always willing to help people with computer problems."

"Like me," Mary said with a grin.

"Like you. I told her she should charge people, because some people take advantage of her."

An idea began forming in Mary's head. "Well, she's a little young, but she's so smart and capable, maybe she should. A freelance business or something like that. Her parents would need to set things up for her, legally and taxwise, but it's doable since she's of legal working age."

Bea's eyes widened. "Do you really think so? She's still in high school."

"Lots of high school students work. Why not computer work? It would probably pay better than flipping burgers at a fast-food joint. And it might help take her mind off of anything that's getting her down at school."

"Hmm." Bea looked surprised but not resistant to Mary's suggestion. "I could talk to her and her parents about it."

Mary shrugged. "I don't know if that would work out for her, but it might help her feel better about herself. She got a huge boost in her confidence just by helping me."

Mary hoped it would help Megan. She'd come to know the girl more over the past few days, and Megan's loneliness at school tugged at her heart. If Megan was able to use her brilliant computer skills for others, it might help her feel better about herself now that she wasn't in the computer club.

"Thanks, Mary," Bea said. "That's a good suggestion."

"No problem. I've come to care for Megan too."

"So what can I help you with today?"

"I'm looking for old property maps for Ivy Bay," Mary said. "Specifically, what was current in 1870. Do you have anything like that?"

"I think so, but just to warn you, it's not well organized. It's all down in the basement."

"Not organized at all?" Mary had visions of being down in the basement for days, looking for the right property records.

"There might be some faint semblance of order," Bea said drily as she peered at Mary over the top of her reading glasses. "You didn't happen to bring a flashlight with you, did you?"

"No."

"You can borrow mine." Bea grabbed one from under the counter and handed it to Mary. "As far as I know, the property maps are all in one place, but I'm not entirely sure where that is in the basement. So when you're poking around, if you find a map, then you know you've found them all."

"Well, that's easier than having them scattered throughout the basement. Thanks, Bea." Mary headed down to the basement, with the musty old-books smell getting stronger as she descended the stairs. The air also cooled slightly, with a faint dampness to it.

When she turned on the light, the fluorescent lighting came to life. She remembered the last time she'd been in here, looking at property records, and how Bea had joked about how there was so much dust and dirt here that they ought to put in brighter lights and grow hydroponic tomatoes! She was again struck by how the basement was much more spacious than she would have expected and was glad, since the dungeon-like space could have been so much more claustrophobic.

The basement was jam-packed with boxes and shelving, all of it stuffed to the gills with old records from the nineteenth century and older. When the records had been transferred from the building housing her bookshop to this building, the county clerk's office had made an attempt to keep records in some semblance of order, but Mary knew she'd still have to do some careful searching.

She decided to start on the shelving because she reasoned that the property maps would be too large for the file boxes that were stacked in the corners and against the walls. Luckily, there were only three shelves that ran along one wall of the basement, so Mary started at one end and worked her way down.

It took her about thirty minutes of carefully peering at each item on the shelf. She was glad she had the flashlight because the shelf above cast a shadow, and the documents were faded and delicate from age. She heard an air-conditioning unit kick in and realized that must be to keep the antique items from being destroyed by the sea air.

She finally found some new cardboard tubes, long and sealed at each end. She took them to a table at the center of the basement and carefully opened one of the tubes. Inside was an old parchment neatly rolled up between two sheets of acid-free archival paper.

She could smell the tang of old ink as she removed the top protective archival paper and saw that the parchment beneath was a map of Ivy Bay from the seventeenth century. It looked like she'd found the maps section. Now to find the right map.

She used her flashlight to look carefully at each tube, but some weren't labeled with the contents, and she had to open them to find out which maps they held. It seemed to take her a long time, but when she looked at her watch, she saw that it was only forty-five minutes since she'd entered the basement.

Then she found the map. The cardboard tube housing it was dated 1860, so Mary eagerly opened it up and placed the map on the table.

She had brought the book with her and now opened it up to the right chapter. According to the biographer, Elias Cowper had hidden in a fisherman's shanty that had a root cellar. No one knew about the root cellar, which was why the sheriff hadn't found him.

Did shanties normally have root cellars? Mary didn't think so. Whoever built the shanty must have been a bit eccentric to have one built.

She looked at the map and compared it with the description in the book. The shanty was in the midst of a cluster of them, right near the docks. Elias Cowper's shanty had been under a big oak tree. Mary sighed. Not very descriptive.

But when she looked at the map, she realized there weren't a cluster of shanties near the docks. There were a few scattered along the beach on either side of the docks, which was smaller than they were today, she noted.

The map was dated 1860, so perhaps the shanties hadn't been built yet. But before she closed up the map, she noticed that there was a large estate near the docks that wasn't there now. The map detailed it as Captain Gregory Gibbs's house. There was a root cellar set a few yards away from the house.

Mary kept searching and finally found a map from 1910. She opened it up and saw that now there was a cluster of shanties built right near the docks, which had expanded from the 1860 map. But the map didn't detail which shanty had a root cellar. Mary had been hoping it would. The townspeople hadn't known about the root cellar back in 1870, but surely someone would have made sure it was on a map forty years later, especially after it had enabled a bank robber to escape the authorities? Apparently not.

That root cellar in the 1860 map nagged at her. The maps didn't detail the transfer of land and how the land had gone from Captain Gregory Gibbs to whoever built the shanties by 1870. For that, she'd have to find property sales records.

Well, she was in the right place to find them.

She was about to start searching the boxes manually but then remembered that Bea had digitized some records and they were searchable. So she headed upstairs.

"Found what you needed?" Bea asked.

"Sort of. I have two questions. First, I need to check the birth and death records of a Captain Gregory Gibbs."

"That's easy." Bea got up and headed to the computer. The birth and death records were digitized and searchable. "Gibbs?"

Mary nodded.

Bea tapped on the keys of the ancient computer, which whirred loudly, protesting the work it had to do. Finally, they found Gregory Gibbs.

"Born in 1800," Bea said, peering at the computer, "and died in 1840. It says he died in a big storm that year."

But the property had still been on the map in 1860, and it still had Captain Gibbs's name on it. "Does it say who inherited his property? His wife or his son?"

"No wife, no son," Bea said. "The obituary mentions a distant cousin, Benjamin Gibbs."

"Can you look up Benjamin Gibbs?"

Bea did, but then shook her head. "We don't have a record. If he's a distant cousin, he might not have been born in Ivy Bay, and if he didn't die here either, then we wouldn't have a record of him."

That made sense. "Any other Gibbs in the records?"

Bea searched, but again shook her head. "Looks like Captain Gibbs was a loner."

"How sad. And he died so young."

"Anyone else you need to look up?" Bea asked. The ancient computer beeped, almost as if in protest, and both women laughed. "Don't worry," Bea said. "The computer's old, but Megan installed the software and said the computer works fine."

Mary said, "How would I find out about property sales? I'd like to find out who bought Captain Gibbs's property."

"What year?"

"Sometime after 1860."

Bea pushed her reading glasses up on her nose. She typed into the computer. "After 1860, you said?"

Mary nodded.

Bea squinted at the computer screen. "The records are in the basement. Well, I figured they would be. Boxes fourteen through sixteen are 1850 to 1900."

"That's perfect. The boxes are numbered?" Mary turned back toward the basement stairs.

"Those boxes should be along the wall to the left of the stairs, if I remember correctly," Bea said.

When Mary took a closer look at the boxes Bea had pointed out, she realized that they were archival-quality boxes. She found box fourteen and set it on the table in the middle of the basement and opened it up.

The records had been stored flat in protective envelopes, but they were labeled. She opened envelopes holding the property records for 1860 and started reading.

She found what she was looking for relatively quickly. In 1869, the property of Captain Gregory Gibbs was sold by Benjamin Gibbs of Boston, which Mary now knew was his distant cousin. The land was sold to the town of Ivy Bay to build the shanties. There were a few notes about the property—mostly that the house had been in severely damaged condition due to flooding damage in 1840 and neglect since then because the house had stood unoccupied. The town was going to tear down the house, and so the land was sold at a lower price.

Ah, now Mary could guess what had happened. Captain Gibbs died in that storm of 1840, and his house was flooded, being so close to the water. But since Benjamin didn't sell the property until 1869, it looked like he hadn't bothered to fix it up, much less live in it, for almost thirty years. The neglect would make the house too damaged to live in, which was why the town bought the land to destroy the house.

What she could guess was that when the town built the shanties, they hadn't known about the root cellar. They obviously hadn't been interested in the blueprints of the house because they were going to tear it down anyway.

Mary went back to the map of 1860 and took a photo of it without using the flash on her camera, so it wouldn't damage the old document. Then she rolled the map back up again between the sheets of archival paper and returned it to its storage tube. She'd get a modern map of Ivy Bay and try to pinpoint the exact location of the root cellar, knowing that a fisherman's shanty would be built right over it.

She put away all the documents she'd been reading and headed up the stairs. After being down there for over an hour, the smell of the old papers was heavy in her lungs, and she would be glad to breathe the air outside the building.

Before she left, she stopped at the front counter. "Thanks so much for all your help, Bea."

"Sure. I hope you found what you were looking for."

"I did. I also was curious. Did anyone else request to look at the property maps sometime in the past week? Or did anyone request access to the archives in the basement?"

"I can check the activity log. That reminds me, I need to log you in too."

"Activity log?" Mary looked in surprise at Bea. "You have an activity log?"

"Sure. I keep an activity log for reporting to the town council about the use of the archives down in the basement, to justify the climate-control system."

Mary remembered the air-conditioning that had kicked in while she was down there. It must be expensive to maintain the temperature and humidity in the old basement for all the records. "I never noticed you keeping a log!" Mary said.

Bea winked. "Honey, I'm a regular James Bond."

Mary chortled. "I guess you are, since I've been coming in here for months and never knew about it. Do you mean you write down everyone who comes to you for help?"

"No, just people who go down into the basement," Bea said. She opened a drawer, then paused. "I forgot...I gave the log to the town council last week for this quarter's reporting."

Mary's anticipation flagged. "When could you get the activity log back? I'd really like to know who else might have requested to see the property maps."

"The town council should be done with it by now. I'll call a council member and ask them to drop it by this afternoon or tomorrow. In the meantime..." Bea pulled out a notebook and wrote Mary's name down, plus the date and "property maps" on the line. Mary thanked Bea again and then escaped to the crisp, clean ocean air outside the building. She headed back to her store.

She wondered who had first figured out the root cellar was under the shanty. Had it been Elias Cowper, or had someone told him about it? Whoever found it must have done so by accident, because by the time the shanties were put up, the root cellar would have been grown over. They probably accidentally—or perhaps on purpose—pulled up a few boards from the floor and found the entrance to the root cellar underneath.

Mary just didn't know if it was all still there.

FOURTEEN

Mary was returning to the bookstore from the county clerk's office when she saw Jerry Avakian leave the ice-cream parlor, without his wife, and stalk down the street. He had a frustrated look on his face that Mary recognized—her late husband, John, had worn that exact same look when the two of them had had a disagreement in public and didn't want to draw attention to it. Had Jerry and Patricia fought?

Passing her bookstore, Mary walked down to the ice-cream parlor. Jerry was on the opposite side of the street, and he didn't see her—instead, he continued blindly down Main Street.

As Mary crossed the street to Bailey's Ice Cream Shop, she saw through the front window that Patricia sat by herself at a table, and it looked like she was trying to hold back tears.

Mary's heart went out to her, and she approached her softly. "Patricia? Are you all right?"

Patricia seemed startled to suddenly see Mary in front of her. She made an effort to compose herself. "I'm fine, thanks," she said in a thick voice.

Mary hesitated, then went to grab some napkins from the table at the side of the store and returned to Patricia's table, setting the napkins in front of her.

The sight of the tissues seemed to crumble Patricia's composure, and her bottom lip trembled.

"You're not all right," Mary said as she sat across from Patricia. "I don't want to embarrass you, but I do want to make sure you'll be okay."

There were only a couple of other people in the ice-cream shop, and Tess Bailey's daughters Paige and Jamie working behind the counter, politely pretended they didn't notice one of their patrons crying at a table. Mary scooted her chair around to try to block the people in the store from seeing Patricia's face.

Patricia took a napkin and wiped her eyes and nose. "Thank you."

"I happened to see you here, and Jerry leaving in a bit of a huff. It reminded me of when John and I had tiffs in public. So I came inside in case you needed help or just a listening ear."

Patricia cried quietly for a few minutes. Then she said, "Th-thank you."

"Just let me know if there's anything I can do for you. Did you want me to drive you home? Or there's a quiet area in my bookstore where you can rest and have a cup of tea."

Patricia didn't answer for a long time. Then she raised watery eyes to Mary. "C-could I go... to your store?"

"Absolutely."

Mary walked Patricia down the street to her bookstore, but for once, she was dismayed to see a customer inside. She hoped the customer would be too distracted in choosing a book to notice Patricia's red nose and puffy eyes. She was even more grateful than normal to Rebecca, because the young woman took one look at Patricia's face, then engaged the customer in conversation so he didn't even see that someone else had entered the store. Mary and Patricia made their way to the reading area at the back.

Mary sat Patricia in one of the armchairs and also set a box of tissues on the coffee table. "I'll be right back with some tea for you."

By the time Mary came back with some tea, Patricia seemed calmer. She accepted the warm cup with a ghost of a smile. "Thank you."

Mary sat in the armchair across from her. "The tea will put a little color back in your cheeks." Patricia opened her mouth to speak, but Mary said, "You don't have to talk, if you don't want to. Everything will be all right," she said.

Her words and tone seemed to help Patricia relax more, although the anxiety never quite left her face. They sat in silence for a long time, and when Patricia finished her tea, Mary immediately made more for her.

When Mary brought her second cup of tea, she sat back down in the armchair and asked Patricia, "I noticed at the library that you like historical novels. What's your favorite time period?"

A little color came back into Patricia's face. "My favorite is the Gilded Age, but there aren't many books set there."

"Cara Lynn James writes romantic novels set in the Gilded Age," Mary said.

"Oh?" Patricia perked up. "I hadn't heard about her." Her dark eyes shone. Mary recognized the excited look of a reader finding a new author.

"They're not mysteries, so I don't carry them here, but I've read them and they're wonderful. Do you read romances?"

"Oh yes," Patricia said. "I'll have to look her up. I usually read Civil War novels since there are so few set in the Gilded Age."

"I love the twenties," Mary said. "Maybe because Agatha Christie's earlier works and most of Dorothy Sayers's mysteries were set in the twenties and thirties."

"I loved *The Great Gatsby*," Patricia said, "but I'm not much into mysteries, so I haven't read much Agatha Christie or Dorothy Sayers. I like fiction, especially historical romances."

"I know another author you might like. Have you read Grace Livingston Hill?"

Patricia shook her head.

"Her earlier books are set in the Gilded Age," Mary said excitedly. She loved conversations like this, matching readers with books. "She wrote from the late 1880s until the late 1940s. Some of her books have a light mystery thread, but many of them were simply romances. The time period is wonderfully authentic when you read her novels."

A smile now spread across Patricia's face. "I had no idea there were other authors who wrote in the Gilded Age. I'm so glad I talked to you."

"I love talking books," Mary said. "I like it so much that for a long time, I was a librarian. Best job for 'talking books' on earth."

"I thought about being a librarian once," Patricia said.

"Did you?"

"But Jerry had the chance to buy the copy and print shop from the previous owner. He had worked for the copy shop

for years, and he's always wanted to own his own business."
Patricia shrugged. "There just wasn't time for me to go back
to school."

"Since the print shop is doing well, maybe you can do
that now?" Mary suggested.

But at Mary's words, Patricia grew sad. "I don't know if
we can afford it now."

Mary wanted to ask her what she meant, but didn't want
to pry, so she remained quiet, trying to be supportive and not
intrusive into Patricia's feelings. But Patricia's words seemed
to clearly indicate they were having financial difficulties.
Perhaps that's why Jerry was talking to Steve at the back of
the bank, and it didn't have anything to do with the robbery?
Or, on the flip side, did their financial problems give them
motivation to have been involved in the robbery?

Patricia cleared her throat and asked, "So what brought
you to the library yesterday? It seems odd to think you'd need
to go to a library when you're surrounded by books." She gave
a small smile.

Mary laughed. "You'd be surprised how often I go to
the library. I have only mystery novels and local books here
at the store, so I go to the library for everything else."

"Oh, of course. I guess I should have realized that. What
books were you looking for?"

"I was hoping the library had a copy of a book I lent to a
friend, but unfortunately, it was misshelved."

Patricia grimaced. "I hate it when that happens. There was
a sequel to a book I'd just finished, and I went to the library
to check it out, but while the computer said the book was on
the shelf, it wasn't. It took the librarian a month before she

found it. I was so impatient to read it that I would have just tried to buy it, but it was out of print and hard to find."

"I'm impressed she found it at all," Mary said. "It's notoriously hard to find books once they've been misshelved. You usually only find them if someone shelving books happens to discover the misshelved book out of place."

"Couldn't you ask your friend to just give you back the book?" Patricia asked. "Who did you lend it to?"

Mary hesitated, then answered slowly, "It was Steve. And now that he's missing..."

Patricia took another sip of tea, then said, "I wish the police would find Steve. I have such a hard time believing he'd rob the bank. There must be some explanation for why he's gone."

"You know, I was thinking that too," Mary said.

Patricia stared at her cup. "I know all the evidence is against him, but it isn't like Steve at all."

"Steve has worked for the bank for years, and he seemed to love his job and the community. In fact, he said that's why he wanted to do the robbery reenactment. He thought it would be fun for the bank customers."

"That sounds like Steve."

Mary sighed. "But if he didn't do it, I'm afraid for him. What happened to him?"

Worry clouded Patricia's face. "I feel so bad for Steve." Mary nodded and was about to say something when Patricia went on, almost as if to herself, "First the bank might close.... Then Jerry's negligence in paying back his loan—" Patricia stopped abruptly and looked up at Mary with a guilty expression.

"You can trust me," Mary said warmly. She meant it, although she was nervous to hear what Patricia meant about the loan.

Patricia looked like she might cry a little more. "We've... we've been having some financial problems lately."

"I'm so sorry," Mary said.

Patricia retreated back into silence, which allowed Mary's mind to whirl about in her shock. Jerry owed the bank money. That must be why he was selling his boat—to pay back his loan to the bank. It also explained why he was willing to sell it for less than its value.

Now, Jerry's words to Steve made more sense to Mary. "*If you weren't being so stubborn about the money...*"

Jerry must have been trying to get Steve to give him more leniency on his loan. That's what he'd meant about Steve being stubborn. But Mary knew Steve. He had probably given Jerry a great deal of leniency and now couldn't give him any more. After all, Steve had to answer to Owen Cooper and maybe the Neels Banking Group for any defaulted loans.

Jerry hadn't robbed the bank, after all. If he had, he wouldn't need to sell his boat to pay back the loan.

But if Jerry didn't commit the robbery, then who did?

———

Just before Patricia left the shop, she took Mary's hand and pressed it tightly. "Thank you. I've felt so alone in all this, but now, it's comforting knowing that someone cares for us."

After she left, Mary turned to Rebecca. "Thanks for distracting that customer the way you did."

"I could see she was upset. I'm glad you were there to help her."

"I hope I helped enough. Talking, and making tea, seems so useless sometimes when someone is hurting."

"I think it made a huge difference for her to have a place of peace for a few minutes," Rebecca said earnestly. "I think that's what you've done your best to create here, in this bookshop."

Mary looked around at the shelves of books, the cozy corner for reading, the playful children's nook. "If a place of peace is what people need, then I'm glad this shop is here to provide it." In fact, the place was very quiet right now. "Where's Ashley?"

"Probably sleeping in the bathtub. She didn't sleep much last night because of her tooth, and she was pretty tired from the visit to the dentist this morning."

Mary had already left Rebecca to handle the shop by herself for most of the afternoon, but she still felt a sense of urgency when it came to finding out about Steve. She wanted to visit the old shanty that Elias Cowper had used. Maybe it was where the robber stashed the loot from the bank. Or maybe it was where the robber had tied up Steve and kept him captive while the police searched for him. She just knew this had to be an important clue.

She turned to Rebecca. "I still have another errand I need to run. Will you be all right here?"

Rebecca grinned. "You sure have a lot of errands to run the past few days. Maybe it has something to do with the bank robbery?"

Mary winked at her. "I'll never tell."

"Go have fun catching villains and saving the world."

Mary went home to get a current map of Ivy Bay and her car so she could drive to the docks. She could perhaps have walked, but she wanted plenty of time to search for the shanty.

When she arrived home, she called out for Betty, but her sister was apparently not back yet from her outing with her grandchildren. Mary got the map of Ivy Bay and then took her camera and hooked it up to her laptop to transfer the photo of the 1860 map. Carefully comparing the two, she circled an approximate area where she thought the shanty would be today. She realized that the shanty might be locked and hoped she wouldn't be disappointed, or else all her hard work today was for nothing.

Mary drove to the docks and parked. She made her way to some rows of shanties, her eyes shifting from the map to the little wooden structures.

It took her about fifteen minutes before she finally found the shanty she was looking for. Many of the other shanties were in good repair, with relatively fresh paint and doors firmly locked. However, this shanty had splinters and peeling paint strips on the walls and some faded graffiti at eye level.

The door was obviously warped, and while it wasn't padlocked, it wouldn't open easily when she tugged at the rusty handle.

Okay, she obviously needed to be a bit more persuasive. She took a deep breath and counted to three, then yanked with all her might. Mary's hands ached where they pulled the handle and the metal bit into her skin. She had wedged one foot against the wall and planted the other on the solid ground, and she strained with every muscle in her body, but the door wouldn't budge.

She finally gave up, panting. Her hands were red and stinging, and she rubbed them against her pant legs.

Now what? She stared at the door. *Window, perhaps?*

She moved around to the side of the shanty to see if there was a window she could open. On one wall, the small windows had dirty panes of glass that had been broken, but someone had boarded the shanty up from the inside. Mary took a branch of driftwood that lay on the ground and knocked shards of glass from one of the windowpanes to clear it away. Then she pushed against the board behind the window. It wouldn't move. She knocked at it with the driftwood, but it still wouldn't move away from where it had been nailed to the wall.

Mary went up to the window and peeked through a crack between the board and the edge of the windowpane. While the inside wasn't entirely dark, she couldn't see more than the opposite wall and a dark pit that was the floor.

She headed to the opposite wall of the small building. Here again, the windowpanes had been cracked and boards nailed to the inside to block them. But at the top, one of the boards either hadn't been nailed in properly or someone—perhaps a curious teenager—had knocked it loose from the wall. It was still nailed into the wall near the bottom of the window, but at the top, it angled away.

Again, she used the driftwood to knock the glass shards out of the window, then hit at the loose board. It gave way like a stiff spring. She hit it several times, and each time the wooden board angled farther and farther away from the wall. Finally, she knocked it loose from the nails anchoring it to the bottom of the window and the board clattered to the floor of the shanty. A cloud of dust exploded up and puffed out the broken windows, and Mary jerked away from the gray cloud, which smelled faintly of mold and old rodent droppings. When it cleared, she approached the open window.

With more light shining inside, the shanty looked depressingly dirty. Dust lay thickly on every surface like dark snow, casting a grayish tinge on the graffiti painted on the inside walls. A few weeds had somehow grown up through the boards of the floor and then died, leaving spindly stalks sticking up. The inside smelled musty with an old animal scent that made Mary wrinkle her nose.

She had remembered to bring a flashlight, and she shone it into the shanty, sweeping the floor, but didn't see any obvious trapdoor to access the root cellar. It was hard to see because the floor was coated with dirt and dust, but she reasoned that it wasn't going to be hidden like a secret passageway in a CIA compound or something. Since there was no furniture in the shanty, she should be able to see the edges of the trapdoor, but she couldn't see anything that pointed to a root cellar.

The air of neglect made Mary realize that no one could have come to the shanty anytime in the past few days and gone inside, or there would have been footprints on the dusty floor. Did that mean no one went into the root cellar? And if no one else went into the cellar, did she really want to go inside it?

She'd been on several exciting treasure-hunting expeditions, but she was beginning to see that not all of them were quite as fun.

She'd give the front door one more try. Mary went around the shanty to the front, grabbed the door handle, and gave a hard, fierce yank.

Maybe her previous efforts had loosened it, because it nudged open a little. Only half an inch, but it was on its way there.

She gave another hard, quick pull, and the door opened another quarter inch. At her third yank, the door shot open with a groan from the warped wood, and Mary had to step back to catch her balance.

The inside of the shanty was even worse with the light from the open doorway shining through. Gigantic cobwebs draped from the low ceiling like swathes of fabric. The old animal smell was stronger and sharper inside, although the smell began to dissipate with the fresh air blowing through the uncovered window and the open door. However, the breeze also kicked up the thick dust, and Mary covered her mouth and nose with her hand.

Mary cautiously entered and shone her flashlight on the floorboards. She had to use her feet to shift aside trash and leaves so she could see the floorboards clearly, but no matter how much she searched—with much coughing from the dust—she couldn't see where the trapdoor might be. Even if two edges of it were flush with the edges of two boards, and the third edge next to a wall, there still should have been a line that cut through two or more boards to form the fourth side of the trapdoor, and she couldn't find anything like that.

Then she remembered what her favorite detectives always did in mystery novels—she began stamping on the floor to see if there was a difference in sound. She stamped all over the shanty floor, but the sound was the same no matter where she stamped.

There wasn't a trapdoor at all.

Mary escaped the shanty into the fresh air, shaking out her hair and clothes. She didn't understand. Was this the shanty that was built over the root cellar? The book had described it as being right at the base of an oak tree, and this was the only shanty with a tree behind it. Mary studied the shanty and the land around it. There were shanties built on either side, several feet apart, giving it a decent space between buildings. Behind the shanty, perhaps two or three feet away, stood the oak tree. The tree stood on a slight rise of ground that sloped down on all sides of it, and the shanty might have been a bit slanted itself because of the ground.

Wait a minute. The tree was on a rise of ground...

Mary reached into her purse for the book on Elias Cowper and again looked at the passage about the root cellar. He'd described it as "a hovel guarded by an oak tree with a root cellar."

She couldn't believe she hadn't noticed it before. The description didn't say specifically that the root cellar was under the shanty or that Elias Cowper had entered the root cellar from inside the shanty. She'd simply assumed as much because of the vague way Elias had described it.

Mary rushed to the back of the shanty and began pulling at the weeds that grew thickly there. Even though most of them were dead, she didn't expect them to come loose easily, but she was astounded when her first handful yanked up a gigantic batch that exposed the ground beneath.

Except it wasn't ground under the weeds. It was a trapdoor made of thick, weathered boards set into the ground slanting from the oak tree. She'd found it.

She began ripping at the weeds in earnest, but again Mary was surprised that the weeds were already loose—as if they'd been torn up, then simply gathered back over the trapdoor.

Someone had been here before her.

Mary didn't expect to see the original rope or ring to pull the trapdoor up, thinking that after over a hundred years, it had probably rotted away, but she pulled a handful of weeds that uncovered a brand-new rope lying against the wood. It had been threaded through a hole in the trapdoor that might have been the base of a metal ring used to pull the door up. The rope had been run under the edge of the trapdoor in order to pull it up, which made the trapdoor crack open where the rope propped it away from the ground.

Someone had definitely been here recently, and then left, covering the trapdoor back up with the pulled-up weeds. At least she knew that person was no longer here, but what would she find in the root cellar? She hated going into the basement at her store, and the thought of the unknown root cellar filled her with dread that wriggled in her stomach like a nest of centipedes. But she grabbed the rope with a trembling hand and tugged the trapdoor open.

It didn't open easily, so it hadn't been used too often in the past few days despite the new rope. The yawning dark hole had only a slightly musty smell like potatoes and was nowhere near as foul smelling as the shanty had been. Some steps made of stone led down into the darkness. Mary also saw some broken cobwebs along the edges of the hole. She could only hope that whoever had been here before her got rid of all the spiders.

Mary shone her flashlight into the hole, took a deep breath, and then crouched low to duck under the edge of the cellar doorway and walk down the stairs. She aimed her flashlight ahead of her so she'd have no surprises or missteps on the narrow stairs. The stone under her feet was solid, however, and slightly worn on the edges from feet walking up and down many years ago. The steps also had some dust, so whoever had been here before hadn't gone up and down enough to sweep the stone clear of dust.

The walls of the root cellar had been fitted with crudely shaped bricks, and some bricks had fallen loose from the walls and crumbled on the floor. Through the holes left by the bricks, tendrils of tree roots curled out from the wall like strands of a woman's hair.

She paused at the base of the steps and swept her flashlight around the space. Wooden shelves had been fitted against some of the walls, but several of them had rotted through and lay in splintered masses on the floor. Others hung crookedly from the wall. But other than the remains of a broken glass canning jar on the floor, the cellar was empty of anything but dirt and bricks.

Mary was about to step onto the floor, but then paused and swept her flashlight over it. There was a thick layer of dust, but curiously, no footsteps were visible. There was a small area at the base of the last step that looked like it had been disturbed recently, but whoever had come into the cellar before her hadn't walked around in it.

Mary stepped down from the last step and started across the floor, shining her light in the farthest corners. She twisted to check behind the stairs, but there was only more broken shelves against the stone of the steps. She looked through the entire cellar but didn't find anything there, no indication that the robber had ever been there.

She headed back up the stairs. Had the robber stashed the loot here right after the robbery and then took it away already? No, the floor didn't look disturbed. It didn't look like anyone had been inside the cellar.

The air as she climbed out the cellar smelled as sweet as lavender. Mary took a deep breath, not realizing until that moment that she'd been breathing shallowly down in the cellar.

She shut the root-cellar door, and she looked around at the weeds she'd cleared away from the top of it. She may as well put the weeds back. She didn't want vandals finding the root cellar.

As she did so, she noticed that while most of them were dead, there were a few green stalks among the dead ones. Whoever had pulled these weeds up and then piled them back on the trapdoor had done this recently if the weeds were still green. Perhaps within a day or two. Since the robbery? Then a thought occurred to her. Maybe it had been the police who were here before. They might have found the book she lent to Steve after all and went to find the shanty. But Mary thought that Chief McArthur would have told her if the police had found the book. Also, the cellar hadn't looked as if many people had been down there, and wouldn't police be more thorough in searching someplace?

She grabbed some more weeds to push back over the root-cellar door, and her eyes caught something shiny in the grass. She flicked aside some blades of greenery.

She recognized the item immediately. It was a pretty pearl earring, in a design similar to what she'd seen on the coffee table in the house of Sandra Rink.

FIFTEEN

———◆◆◆———

Mary drove to the bookshop and parked her car. But as soon as she entered the shop, Rebecca took one look at her and dropped her jaw. "What happened to you?"

Mary sighed. "I had a skirmish with a root cellar."

"Looks like the root cellar won."

Ashley wandered out from the children's nook, yawning and rubbing her eyes. But when she saw Mary, her eyes became as wide as saucers. "Wow, Mrs. Fisher, you look like you were playing in a sandbox or something."

"What were you doing in a root cellar?" Rebecca asked.

"I promise to tell you later, but right now I feel absolutely disgusting."

"You're going straight home to a hot shower," Rebecca announced. "I can close up the shop."

"Thanks."

Betty had a reaction similar to Rebecca's when Mary walked through the front door of their home. "Good gracious! Did you get into a fight?"

Mary laughed. "Ashley thought I'd been playing in a sandbox, but my own sister asks if I've been in a brawl?"

Betty gave a rueful smile. "Well, you must admit you look worse for wear. What happened?"

Mary bent to release Gus from his carrier, and he streaked away as if he were offended by her shanty-and-root-cellar odor. "I got my hands on a copy of the historical book I lent to Steve and found out that there was a root cellar near a fisherman's shanty that the original robber used in 1870 to hide out. I went looking for the root cellar."

"Root cellar?" Betty's voice took on a strident note. "Off to the shower with you right away."

Mary took her time in the shower. She had thought maybe the loot from the safe-deposit boxes would be in the root cellar. It would have been the perfect place to hide it. The sheriff in 1870 hadn't known about it, and it was so overgrown and forgotten that the police today wouldn't have known about it either. At least not right away.

But anyone who read the book would know about it, and she couldn't think that anyone would bother to go searching for that root cellar unless they intended to use it to hide something.

Finding Sandra's earring had disturbed her. It meant Sandra had been at the root cellar—and recently. Mary could guess that Sandra knew about the root cellar because she borrowed the book from Steve, read about the root cellar, then went to find it. Or perhaps Steve had found the root cellar and told her about it.

But why would she or Steve go looking for the root cellar? She could believe Sandra would borrow the book for the reenactment, but she or Steve wouldn't need to look up the root cellar for the reenactment.

And to top it off, it seemed odd Sandra or Steve would go through the trouble of finding the root cellar and then not go inside.

Did Sandra have the historical book Mary had lent to Steve? If she did, why hadn't she turned it in to the police? She would have known that the reenactment was based on the book. Maybe she didn't think the book was an important lead and didn't bother telling anyone about it.

The root cellar had no part in Monday's reenactment, but because of its connection to the original robbery, it could have a connection to the robbery from a couple of days ago—perhaps as a hideaway for the robber the way Elias Cowper had used it. And finding Sandra's earring at the root cellar might connect her, tenuously, to that robbery. When Mary took into account the other mysterious things she'd observed—Sandra not wanting anyone to know someone was staying with her, the passport application...

Mary remembered the man at the pharmacy, and immediately she realized who he looked like: Sandra. Certain things about his features were masculine versions of Sandra's face. Was he a brother? a cousin? Mary also guessed he was the person staying at Sandra's house, who smoked those cigarettes. If he were a relative, it would explain why she'd allow someone who smoked to stay at her place, when she was asthmatic. But why had she seemed to want to hide the fact he was staying with her?

Suddenly, Mary remembered what Sherry Walinski had said about Sandra and the girls she coached in volleyball, something that Mary hadn't paid much attention to at the time. She knew Sherry would be home from work soon. She had to make sure she spoke to her tonight to ask her about the community center Sandra took the girls to each year. And Mary had a legitimate reason to ask also, because she had been thinking of talking to Sherry about donating those damaged books at her shop to a school library—why not that community center?

Mary felt infinitely better after her shower, and she joined Betty in the kitchen for a cup of tea. She kept her eye on the clock because Sherry usually got home from work a little before the time Mary and Betty had dinner.

"So what did you find in the root cellar?" Betty asked, handing Mary a steaming mug of tea.

"Nothing except dirt and cobwebs."

Betty shuddered. "What in the world were you hoping to find there?"

Mary sighed. "I was hoping for one of two things. One possibility was that I'd find the loot stolen from the bank robbery."

"What? Why?"

"It was just a wild guess. The root cellar was where the original robber in 1870 hid out, and since I'd lent Steve that book for the reenactment, I wondered if maybe he used the root cellar to stash the valuables stolen."

"And what was the other thing?"

"I wondered if maybe I'd find Steve—either hiding out or tied up because the robber hid him away in order to take his place at the reenactment."

Betty sighed, echoing her sister. "I know you don't think he's the robber. I hope he's all right."

"Bets, I'm so worried about him. If he wasn't the robber, then where is Steve? It's been two days since the robbery."

The two of them sat in silence for a few moments. Then Mary said, "Bets, let's pray for him. It's the best thing we can do for him now."

The two of them clasped hands and bowed their heads, each praying for Steve and that the police would find the robber soon.

When they said Amen, Mary felt lighter in her spirit. She had to trust that God would take care of everything. "Thanks, Bets. I feel better."

"I do too."

"So what happened when you went to Jayne's store today?" Betty asked, concern in her eyes.

Mary told her what she'd uncovered about Jayne and the fake clock, and how she wasn't sure if she should talk to Jayne about it.

"Oh, Mary." Betty clasped her hand. "I know you'll figure out what you should do, even if it ends up being something hard."

"Thanks, Bets." Mary sighed. "I'll need to pray about it tonight before I go to bed."

Betty also asked if Mary had discovered anything more about Sandra and Jerry, and so Mary told her about her talk with Patricia Avakian today and also about her need to speak to Sherry tonight about the community center Sandra went to with the girls' volleyball team.

Mary sipped her tea. "Enough about my day. How was the beach with Betsy and Allison?"

Betty chatted about that for a while, but then Mary's eyes fell on the wall clock and she got up. "Excuse me, but Sherry should be home now, and I want to talk with her before she starts dinner. I'll be back in a few minutes."

Mary headed to her neighbor's house. Sherry's car was in the driveway, so Mary knew she was home from her job at the high school.

Sherry answered Mary's knock almost immediately. "Hi, Mary. What's up?" Her green eyes lit up with curiosity.

"I hope I'm not interrupting you in the middle of dinner."

"No, not at all. Did you want to come in for a cup of tea? I just boiled water."

"I'm afraid I can't stay long. I wanted to ask you a question about that community center Sandra takes the girls to every year."

"Sure, what about it?"

"Do you remember the name?"

"Um…Hope Community Center? Or maybe it's Mercy Community Center? Something like that. Why?"

Mary was a bit disappointed not to know the exact name. And if it were a simple name like Hope or Mercy, she'd have a hard time finding it in the Boston phone book. "I have some extra books that are damaged, and I was going to give them away when I remembered you'd mentioned that community center Sandra used to go to. I figured it would be nice to donate to them, since Sandra recommends them."

"Oh, sure. I think Sandra even mentioned something about some book clubs the community center sponsors."

Mary said, "I didn't know Sandra was from Boston until you mentioned that community center the last time we talked."

Sherry's brow wrinkled. "I think she said she was from Boston. I know she went to that Boston community center, so I guess I assumed she grew up there."

"Well, she's part of Ivy Bay now," Mary said with a smile.

"Yep. And thanks for reminding me about her. I think I'll go over to check up on her and see how she's doing."

"I think she'd like that. These last few days must have been stressful for her."

Mary bid Sherry good-bye, and as she walked across the yard back to her house, her thoughts were confused. The woman whom Sherry had described didn't seem like the type of person to rob a bank. Yet why had Sandra been at the root cellar? She had to look up the community center. If she talked to someone there, she might learn more about Sandra.

As she walked into the kitchen, the phone rang. "I'll get it," Mary told her sister, and went to pick it up. "Hello?"

"Hi, Mary. This is Bea Winslow. I'm sorry I didn't get back to you earlier. I got the activity log back, but I didn't get a chance to look at it until now because a council member came by and needed me to do something for him that took most of the afternoon."

"Don't worry about it, Bea. I was busy all afternoon too." Mary had to smile at her own words. "Did you find out who went down to the archive basement in the past few weeks?"

"Yes, I looked through my activity log. Someone did request to look at the old property maps in the basement. It was Steve Althorpe."

"When?"

"It was about two weeks ago, well before the robbery, so I didn't even think to tell the police," Bea said, a note of worry in her voice. "I always get random people asking to see them because Ivy Bay is such a historical town, so I didn't think anything of it. I usually just let people have fun down there."

Mary remembered searching through the records in the musty basement and wouldn't necessarily describe it as having "fun." "He requested to see the property maps? You're sure about that?"

"Yes, I usually write down what people ask to see," Bea said. "It shows that all parts of the archive are in demand, not just a certain set of records."

"Okay. Thanks, Bea."

Mary hung up the phone. She realized that just because Steve asked to see the old property maps didn't automatically mean anything. He'd read the historical book on Elias Cowper in preparation for the reenactment, and it could be that he had gone to the county clerk's office to find the original shanty out of curiosity.

But Sandra, who worked with Steve, had obviously been at the root cellar sometime between the robbery and today. Why?

Could Steve and Sandra really be responsible for the robbery after all?

SIXTEEN

◆◆◆

The next morning, Mary woke up early. She lay in bed for a while, listening to the sounds of birds as the sun rose, letting the peace of the morning soak into her. Then she got up and reached for her Bible.

She was reading Proverbs, and today the verse that caught her eye was in chapter eleven, verse eight: *The righteous person is rescued from trouble, and it falls on the wicked instead.*

She bowed her head to pray. *Dear Lord, I don't know what has happened with the bank, and I can't believe Steve or Sandra would do something like rob it. Won't You please reveal to us the truth and show Your justice? And if Steve is indeed kidnapped or in hiding, please take care of him. Amen.*

Mary went downstairs and, as usual, Betty had been up for a while and was making breakfast. "Good morning. Want some coffee? I'm almost done with the eggs."

"Coffee smells divine." Mary poured herself a cup. "Do you need help?"

"Nope. I'm only making cheese omelets. Go ahead and set the table."

Mary set out plates, forks, and napkins, and poured some orange juice for herself and Betty. Her sister laid the platter of steaming omelets on the table and sat down with her own cup of coffee.

"It's your turn to say grace," Betty said.

Mary closed her eyes and folded her hands. "Dear Lord, thank You for all You've blessed us with. Thank You for our health and this wonderful food. Please guide our day today. Amen."

"Amen." Betty looked up and began serving the omelets onto their plates.

"What are you up to today?" Mary asked her.

"Gardening. The nice weather isn't going to last much longer, and there are a few flower beds I need to prepare for winter."

"Don't work too hard. It's supposed to be rather warm today."

"Are you going to do anything special besides the store?"

"I'm not sure. The day's still young."

"I was reading in the paper this morning that they still haven't found Steve," Betty said with a wrinkle to her brow.

"I hope he's all right," Mary said, "whether he robbed the bank or not. I'm worried about him."

"Me too," Betty said.

They ate in silence for a few minutes. Then Betty said, "I almost forgot. I saw Owen this morning when I went to get the paper. He was out jogging, but he stopped for a minute to say hello. He seemed a little happier today." Betty's eyebrows rose.

"Do you think that means good news about the bank?"

"I asked him, and he naturally said he couldn't say anything about it. But he seemed to be in a much better mood than he's been for a couple of weeks. I can't help but hope it might mean that Neels isn't going to close the bank."

"Oh, Bets, I hope so too."

They finished their breakfast, chatting about the unseasonably warm weather they were supposed to have that day and what Betty wanted to grow in the garden next year.

Mary washed up the breakfast dishes, but her mind was still on the earring she'd found at the root cellar. She couldn't understand why Sandra would go there, but Mary was trying to be sensible and not jump to the conclusion that Steve and Sandra were the robbers. There might be an innocent reason why she was there.

The problem was that it wasn't a place the historical society would be interested in. The only reason she could think of to visit was to hide something there, but then again, it could be to hide something that had nothing to do with the robbery.

Last night, Mary had done an Internet search for Hope Community Center and Boston, and the search engine showed several results, including One Hope Community Center in Michigan and Hope Community Center in Montana. There was also Mountain of Hope Community Center in Boston, but when she clicked on the Web site, the link was broken. She did another search for Mountain of Hope Community Center, and the search engine found a blog post from a year ago that said Mountain of Hope Community Center had closed.

She then tried the other name Sherry gave her: Mercy Community Center. The first result was Mercy Community

Center on Bellevue Street in Boston, so Mary clicked on the community center's Web site and began reading. The community center offered a variety of services for youth in the city, all free of charge. They provided child care for younger children and also clubs and service projects for teens. She clicked through more pages on the Web site and found that the community center was privately funded, plus they had a wealth of volunteers, mostly adults who had been part of the community center when they were younger.

As Sherry had mentioned, they also had book clubs. It gave Mary a perfect reason to call them today.

Betty headed out to the garden just as Mary finished the dishes. She grabbed the phone and then dialed the number she had copied from the contact page of the community center's Web site. She sat at the kitchen table with another cup of coffee while she waited for someone to answer.

"Hello. This is Mercy Community Center," a friendly female voice answered. "Eloise speaking. How may I help you today?"

"Hello, Eloise, my name is Mary Fisher, and I run Mary's Mystery Bookshop in Ivy Bay. I was thinking about perhaps donating some books to your center, but I wanted to find out more about you first."

"Oh, certainly. What would you like to know?"

"Can you tell me about your reading programs?"

"We have wonderful reading programs here. FunRead, our after-school program, is staffed entirely by volunteers, but they're all either schoolteachers or trained through our reading-coach training program. Our success rate is excellent—most children improve their reading grades or scores at school so much that they rank above average for their age group.

"We also have book clubs for teenagers. Our largest book club is the fantasy and science-fiction club, but we also have a mystery book club, a girls' book club and a boys' book club, a young writers' group, and a poetry group. Each club is staffed by one or more adult volunteers, and they meet anywhere from once a month to once a week, depending on the group. Some groups are very large, while others are smaller. We're actually thinking about splitting up the fantasy and science-fiction club because it's so big and holding meetings on different days of the week to accommodate different teens' schedules."

Mary was amazed and impressed. "That's astounding. How did you become so successful with all your book clubs?"

"One of the volunteer teachers in the reading program suggested a book club for the older kids, and it took off from there. There was so much interest that we started forming more and more clubs. But we have many very successful programs—like our sports programs and our mentoring programs—because we have such great volunteers. Most of them used to be kids who went through the community center themselves and had such a positive experience that they want to give back."

"I heard about you through a woman who coaches a club volleyball team here in town, Sandra Rink. She apparently went to your community center when she was growing up in Boston."

"Oh, Sandra! We love Sandra. She brings her volleyball team here once a year to volunteer. We have a trash pickup where we clean up the neighborhood streets once a quarter, and Sandra brings her girls to help out to teach them what community service is about."

"It seems Sandra really loves your community center."

"Oh, she does, but I think she loves your little community even more. We've offered her a job here as program manager several times—we even offered to pay her more than what she makes now at the bank—but she always turns it down. She says she likes Ivy Bay better than Boston."

Mary was confused. If Sandra loved Ivy Bay so much that she turned down a good job at a community center she was fond of, why would she jeopardize her life here in Ivy Bay by robbing the bank? That didn't make sense.

Mary said, "Well, we love Sandra too. I've known her for years. And the parents in Ivy Bay love her for all she does for the teen girls in the community."

"That's so nice to hear. Not all the kids who come through Mercy Community Center turn out so well, and we always love hearing about the ones who go on to live successful, happy lives." Eloise then lowered her voice a tad to say, "We're so glad Sandra turned out better than her brother did. When he was released from prison, we really worried that she'd get sucked in by him again, but she managed to avoid him and make a better life for herself."

Brother. Sandra had a brother, just as Mary suspected. Was the fact he had been in jail the reason Sandra hadn't wanted Mary to know her brother was staying with her? "Yes, I can tell you that she's very happy here and well loved by everyone." Mary went on, "Well, I think you've told me enough about the community center. How should I donate these books?"

Eloise gave her the address to mail them to and said that the community center would send her a tax-deductible receipt if she included a self-addressed stamped envelope. "The mystery book club will be ecstatic," Eloise said. "Thank you so much."

After Mary hung up the phone, she recalled her visit to Sandra's house and everything she'd seen there. Sandra hadn't had any photos displayed of her family—just the volleyball team, the child she was sponsoring, and a photo of her friends. Mary had forgotten about that until now. Maybe she didn't have photos of her brother because she wasn't close to him, or she was embarrassed of him.

What Eloise said about Sandra confirmed what Mary knew about Sandra. She loved Ivy Bay and wouldn't rob the bank.

But her *brother* might.

The way Eloise talked about him, Sandra's brother was bad news, and Eloise had made it seem like he got Sandra involved in some bad business.

Now, the things she had overheard outside of Sandra's house made more sense. She had said, "I'm tired of bailing you out" and "You can't make me help you." Mary now suspected Sandra was talking to her brother. She was so good-hearted, even if she didn't like what her brother got into, that she wouldn't turn him away if he came to town and needed a place to stay. Maybe he was in trouble and she wasn't supposed to tell anyone where he was, which might have been a reason she didn't want Mary to know he was staying with her.

Mary still didn't really know if he was involved in the robbery at all, but Sandra might be intimidated by him or even coerced into helping him. Sandra had started in surprise at the pharmacy—probably at seeing him there in the aisles. Maybe she hadn't expected to see him out and about in Ivy Bay, or maybe his presence there was a threatening gesture to keep her in line.

It still didn't explain why Sandra went to the root cellar but didn't go inside or store anything in there. And if her brother was the robber, then where was Steve?

But if Sandra's brother was the robber and did something to Steve, Mary couldn't believe Sandra would stand by and let him kidnap Steve or hurt him. She'd try to do something about it. Mary guessed that it depended on what Sandra's relationship with her brother was like.

Mary got to her feet, resolve stiffening her spine. There was no way to know that unless she talked to Sandra.

SEVENTEEN

❖◆❖

Mary was walking toward her store, Gus's carrier in her hand. She glanced across the street at Gems and Antiques and saw Jayne through the store window. Jayne was at the counter, her head bowed and shoulders shaking, looking completely miserable.

Mary's heart went out to her. What was wrong? She had been trying to decide if she ought to talk to Jayne about how she was selling the fake clock as a real Paquet, unsure if she had the right to confront her about her actions. But Jayne was her friend, and in seeing her so distressed right now, Mary simply had to see if there was anything she could do to comfort her.

She entered the store tentatively, still holding Gus in his carrier. Jayne sat at the counter, reading something on her computer screen. She didn't look quite as upset as she'd had a moment ago, but she did look like she was trying not to cry.

When Jayne looked up and saw Mary, she tried to compose herself and put on her "customer" smile but didn't succeed very well. "Hi, Mary."

"I saw you across the street when I was walking to my store," Mary said in a low, gentle voice. "Are you all right?"

Jayne's shoulders sagged, and her stress and worry etched deep lines in her brow.

"You don't have to tell me," Mary went on, "but I just want to know if there's anything I can do for you, Jayne."

"Thank you," Jayne said in a whisper. "I'm just upset about something."

"Can I help at all?"

At those words, Jayne's face crumpled. "It's been a horrible two weeks," she said in a broken voice and reached below the counter, bringing out a box of tissues.

"Oh, Jayne." Mary set Gus's carrier down on the floor, then went around the counter to put her arm around her friend.

"I'm a terrible person." Jayne cried into her tissues. "I'm a liar."

Mary knew Jayne was crying about lying about the clock, but Mary also wanted to extend God's grace to Jayne. "Jayne, none of us is perfect. We just need to make things right when we make a mistake."

"This wasn't a mistake. I did it on purpose." Jayne sobbed into her tissues for a few minutes while Mary patted her back.

Mary realized she should have known that Jayne's incredibly good nature would eventually win out over any bad decisions she might have made. "I'm sure if you just determine to do what's right, everything will turn out okay," Mary said in a soothing voice.

Jayne sniffed. "I sold that clock today." She gestured to the antique clock with the Not for Sale sign.

Mary was silent, letting Jayne talk. She knew that selling the clock wasn't the good thing it would normally have been.

Jayne shook her head, tears falling down her cheeks. "Oh, Mary, I lied about it. I said it was from a certain clockmaker, but it's not."

Mary hesitated, then said, "That's so unlike you."

"I'm so ashamed. I did it because I was embarrassed and angry. The seller I bought the clock from faked it, but I didn't realize it until I'd brought it home."

"Don't be too hard on yourself. No one's perfect, Jayne."

"I should have seen it," Jayne said. "The seller put an older clock's mechanisms in the framework of a slightly newer one with the paintwork on it. I was more interested in examining the mechanics to determine its age. When I got it home, I realized the seller had blackened over the Blythe-Stewart logo, making it look like an age spot."

"Oh, Jayne," Mary said.

"I had spent so much money for the clock because I thought it was an authentic Paquet and could resell it for much more than what I paid for it. After I got home and realized it was a fake, I tried to contact the seller, thinking he was just mistaken about the clock, but he's mysteriously disappeared and I'm down several thousand dollars." Jayne swiped at her eyes with her crumpled tissue.

"I'm so sorry. This must be a blow to your business."

Jayne hiccuped. "Rich doesn't know about it. I was too embarrassed to tell him." She bit her lip, fighting for composure. "After the bank robbery, he made some comment about how the bank could be so stupid as to be robbed, and I just couldn't tell him."

Mary squeezed Jayne's shoulders.

"At the reenactment, I saw the robber and was so upset and angry at having my money stolen by that seller that I just couldn't stay and watch. I felt like I was being robbed all over again. I went to the back of the bank and cried my eyes out. I didn't want to go back to the store because I was afraid Rich would see me crying and guess what was wrong."

So that was why Jayne had lied about being behind the bank. She'd been embarrassed and upset and trying to hide this secret from her husband, from everyone.

"And then I sold the clock this morning." Jayne's voice came out sounding like a wail. "I don't know why I listed it as a Paquet when I know it's not. This entire time I've been so stressed about it, and I realize I'm feeling guilty about what I'm doing."

"You need to withdraw from the sale," Mary said. "I think once you do that, you'll feel better."

Jayne hesitated, her eyes closed. Then she slowly nodded. "You're right. I know you're right. I just haven't been able to gather up the courage to do the right thing."

"You should tell Rich too," Mary said.

Jayne paled. "What will he think of me? I'm supposed to have known better about that clock. And then to lie to him about it all..."

"We sometimes don't realize until later how important it is to do the right thing," Mary said slowly. "Once, I had learned a truth that would devastate Betty and her family. It would cause them to lose a precious family...heirloom. I didn't want to tell the truth, but I did because it was the right thing to do." Mary was talking about the Emerson gristmill, and how she'd learned that in actuality, it had indeed been sold—sort of—to the Hopkins family.

Mary continued, "Betty was upset at me, but I *had* to do the right thing. It would have been so much worse if I hadn't told Betty and allowed her family to continue to do the *wrong* things because they were ignorant of the truth."

Jayne took a few quick breaths, then said, "You're right. He's out of town today, but I'll tell him tonight."

"I'll be praying for you too," Mary said. "Remember how Psalm 11 says, 'For the Lord is righteous, he loves justice; the upright will see his face'? I just know things will come out all right for you."

Jayne mopped at her face, and Mary rubbed Jayne's shoulder comfortingly. Gus took that moment to mewl.

"I'm sorry," Mary said. "I'd forgotten about poor Gus."

"You should go open your shop," Jayne said. "And I'll e-mail that buyer. And, Mary"—Jayne touched Mary's hand—"thank you."

"Anytime, friend."

Mary picked up Gus's carrier and headed across the street. She was glad that was resolved, and Jayne was going to do the right thing.

Mary opened her store and released Gus to sniff the bookshelves. Her anxiety over Sandra returned, and she waited rather impatiently for Rebecca to arrive.

As soon as Rebecca walked through the door with Ashley, Mary said, "I know you just arrived, but could you please watch the store for me? I need to speak to someone this morning."

Rebecca straightened in surprise, then said, "Sure, Mary. Don't worry about it."

"Thanks." Mary hurried out and crossed the street.

As she walked toward the bank, she was surprised to see the accountant from the Neels Banking Group sitting on a bench outside in the sunlight. The morning had already become quite warm, but what surprised her was that he was licking ice cream from a cone.

He saw her and paused in his eating. A bit of red crept up his neck, but then he nodded to her and gave a half smile.

Mary wanted to get inside the bank to try to speak to Sandra, but his changed demeanor seemed like an invitation. She impulsively went up to him with a friendly smile. "Is that from Bailey's Ice Cream Shop?"

"Yes." He cleared his throat, then said, "Thank you for the recommendation. Their ice cream is indeed quite good."

His stiff and rude demeanor of yesterday was gone, and his face seemed more open and relaxed.

"I'm glad you think so. What flavor did you get?"

"Butter pecan."

"That's a perfect flavor for fall, and today's a good day for eating ice cream. It's warmer than it's been all week."

He nodded but seemed unsure what to say. Mary wondered if he were shy.

"I hope you enjoyed your stay in Ivy Bay this week," she said. "Did you get a chance to visit other restaurants here?"

"Er... no, I haven't had time."

"Maybe you can visit Sam's Seafood today."

"I'm afraid not. I'm leaving this morning."

"That's too bad." Mary gestured to his ice cream. "I see, now. That's breakfast, is it?"

He gave a rueful half smile. "I wanted to try it before I left."

"I hope you had a good visit here."

"Yes, I did."

Mary wondered if his words and his nicer attitude meant that the bank wasn't going to close. She didn't know him or his attitude about the bank, so she couldn't know if he would be happy because the bank wasn't going to close or because it was. Then again, maybe he wasn't here to assess the financials of Ivy Bay Bank & Trust at all.

At that moment, the front doors of the bank opened, and Sandra came out. Mary's heart quickened. She couldn't miss this opportunity to speak to her. She turned to the accountant. "It was nice meeting you. Have a good day."

"Thank you. You too."

Mary hurried to intercept Sandra, who was heading to the bank's parking lot. Sandra's face was ghostly, and her eyes had dark smudges under them. She caught sight of Mary and hesitated, then turned away, hurrying away from her.

However, Mary caught up with her. "Sandra, I'm so glad I saw you. Could I please speak to you?"

"I'm sorry, Mary, but I was about to leave." Sandra didn't look at Mary.

"I really do need to speak to you."

"Why don't you come by my house later tonight?"

"I don't think it would be good to wait." Mary didn't really want to bring this subject up here, in the middle of the parking lot.

"I need to run an errand that's very important."

"Sandra," Mary said softly, "it's about your brother."

Sandra froze.

"I know you must love him," Mary went on, "but if something has happened to Steve—"

"I don't know what's happened to Steve," Sandra whispered. "He won't tell me." A tear rolled down her cheek.

Mary immediately stepped closer to her, touching her shoulder.

Sandra fished a tissue out of her purse and dabbed at her eyes. "I was going to the police station to tell them the little I know."

"What do you know?"

Sandra sighed and looked as if she were going to cry some more, but she took a deep breath and held back her tears. "My brother Jesse is staying with me. He didn't want anyone to know he was in Ivy Bay, but he didn't tell me why. I think he's hiding from the law—maybe he did something in Boston—but he wouldn't tell me. You have to believe me." Sandra looked at Mary with desperate eyes. "I didn't know he was going to rob the bank."

"I believe you," Mary said.

"When he first came to Ivy Bay, I let him stay with me because I promised our mother I would always help my baby brother whenever he needed it, but I didn't like having him in the house. He's always been trouble, and he came in the middle of the night, unexpectedly, which made me think he wasn't up to any good. He said he wasn't in any trouble, but..." Sandra sighed heavily.

"I can understand why it would be hard to trust him."

"I should have been smarter," Sandra said fiercely. "I should have known he'd take advantage of a situation if he thought he could get away with it. Steve had talked to me about the robbery reenactment and even gave me that book you lent him, so Jesse knew all about it. And then at the robbery, it took me a little while, but I began to suspect that it wasn't Steve but Jesse in Steve's place. That's why, after the robber left, I hurried back to the safe-deposit vault. I just knew something was wrong."

"It's good that you did. Poor Owen would have been tied up longer if you hadn't."

"I suspected the robber had been Jesse, but I didn't have any proof. I tried to get him to talk to me, but he kept stonewalling me. I was mostly worried about Steve."

"You don't know what Jesse did with him?"

Sandra shook her head miserably. "I asked him dozens of times, but he wouldn't tell me. He said I shouldn't worry about him. I begged him not to hurt Steve, so Jesse promised not to."

Mary's swallowed. "Do you believe him?"

Sandra paused, then nodded. "I do. The way he said it, I think he'll make sure Steve is okay. He's never hurt anyone as far as I know."

Mary hoped she was right.

Sandra went on, "I kept changing my mind about if I should go to the police with what I suspected about Jesse or if I should just keep helping my brother the way I promised my mother I would. I felt so guilty about either choice. And the longer I waited, the worse it would look for me. I'm sure the police wouldn't believe I didn't immediately recognize my brother at the reenactment, even if I tried to explain that I hadn't seen him very much for the past several years. And he was staying at my house too. It makes me look complicit in the robbery."

"Maybe not if you help the police. And you said you were going to the police station to do the right thing. I hope you'll still do that."

Sandra nodded, grabbing another tissue from her purse and wiping her eyes. "When Jesse was at my house, I was so torn about if I should go to the police and open myself up to suspicion, or if I should continue to help my brother. I loved my mother so much, and she was so earnest when she asked me to promise to help him."

"Even help him escape the law and get yourself in trouble too? Surely your mother wouldn't want you to do that."

"I suppose not. Today, I couldn't stand it anymore and I decided to go tell the police everything I know, even though it isn't much."

"Where's your brother now?"

"I don't know. He's still in town. He didn't leave right after the robbery for some reason—he wouldn't tell me—but some things he said yesterday make me think he's going to leave soon. I haven't seen him since last night."

Her comment about leaving town reminded Mary of the passport. "Were you intending to go with him?"

Sandra blinked at her. "No. Why do you ask?"

"Well, that passport application in your purse..."

Sandra's mouth formed an O. "Oh my goodness. I didn't realize how that would look. I was just so excited for the opportunity...."

"What opportunity?"

"For eight years, I've been sponsoring a child through Mercy's Children, which is an international relief organization for children. They organize missions trips each year, and this year it's to Bolivia, where my sponsored child lives. I didn't find out about it until a week ago, and I applied, and they said there's a spot for me. So I was getting an expedited passport so I could go and meet Pamela in person. It's something I've always wanted to do."

Mary remembered the toothy grin of the child in the photo on Sandra's fridge, and it made perfect sense to her. "You've been sponsoring Pamela for eight years?"

"Ever since she was a baby. We write to each other fairly often." Sandra looked anguished. "I didn't mean to make it look like I was trying to skip town. It really didn't occur to me."

"It wouldn't have occurred to me either."

Sandra quickly mopped at her face with a fresh tissue, then looked at Mary with quiet strength in her gaze. "I think I should go to the police station now."

"Would you like me to go with you?"

Sandra gave a small smile. "I think I'd like that."

Mary kept her arm around Sandra as they walked down the street toward the police station. She felt Sandra trembling as they opened the front glass door of the white concrete-block building, but the young woman spoke in a clear voice to the officer at the front desk. "I need to speak to someone about the bank robbery."

Mary thought that with the seriousness of the robbery, the police would try to see Sandra as soon as possible, but the officer at the reception desk had a blank expression on his face as he said, "Can I have your name please?"

"Sandra Rink. I'm a teller at the bank."

He wrote her name down and said, "We'll call you when we're ready. Please have a seat."

Mary and Sandra sat side by side on some heavy wooden chairs in the small reception area. Sandra stared down at the wide plank floor while Mary gazed at the sage-green walls. Two other people sat in the reception area—an old woman with a gigantic sunflower in her hat and a sullen-looking teen in a black T-shirt and ripped jeans with dyed black hair that slashed across his face in a punk cut.

They waited a good fifteen minutes while the officers called up the old woman and the teen ahead of them. Mary frowned. Shouldn't they speak to Sandra quickly? It was about the bank robbery!

Finally, Deputy Wadell appeared and called out, "Sandra Rink?"

Sandra stood and approached him. Mary followed, but Deputy Wadell gave her an apologetic look. "Sorry, just Ms. Rink."

Mary touched Sandra's shoulder. "I'll be waiting for you here."

But Sandra shook her head. "You've helped me a lot already, Mary. Why don't you go back to your store? I'll be fine."

"Are you sure? I don't mind waiting."

"I'm sure. Thanks for everything." Sandra preceded Deputy Wadell toward the back of the station.

Mary walked out of the station into bright sunlight. She couldn't believe this warm weather at this time of year.

An acrid smell reached her nose, and she turned to see a man leaning against the police-station wall, smoking a cigarette. She was about to walk past him, when an idea hit her.

Mary marched up to him, and he looked startled at her purposeful expression. "Uh, can I help you?"

"I hope so. Where would someone go to buy"—she couldn't remember the name, so she plucked her notebook out of her purse and looked up the name of the cigarette she'd seen in Sandra's apartment—"Veryan Chapp kretek cigarettes? I believe they're clove cigarettes."

"Yeah, they are." The man wrinkled his brown-gray brows and ran a hand down his stringy hair. "They're not that easy to find. I think the only place that sells them is Barnaby's, down by the docks."

"Thank you." As Mary walked away, she took a deep breath to give herself courage. She was out to catch a thief.

EIGHTEEN

※ ◆ ◆ ※

Barnaby's was a seedy shack that looked like it had been upgraded—barely—from a fishing shanty. It sat close to where many of the commercial fishermen berthed their fishing boats, and the ground outside the store was littered with cigarette butts, despite the fact that there was a sand-filled tub right next to the front door to serve as an ashtray. A few men lounged outside of Barnaby's, smoking cigarettes and joking with one another in coarse, hard voices. They glanced at Mary, but then ignored her.

She entered the store and was immediately enveloped in the scent of tobacco and tar. The store was dominated by a counter running through it, with an old cash register sitting on top and a bored-looking young man standing behind it. He flipped his dirty-blond hair out of his eyes as he saw her. "What can I get ya?" he drawled.

"Do you sell Veryan Chapp kretek cigarettes?" she asked.

"Yeah." He absently scratched at his chest, and Mary saw the hole at the armpit of his grimy T-shirt. "How many you want?"

"I don't want to buy any, but I'd like to know who might have bought them in the past week or so."

The clerk's pale-blue eyes narrowed as he regarded her. "Why do you need to know?"

Mary hesitated, then reached into her purse and took out a twenty-dollar bill, sliding it across the counter.

"A bunch of fishermen buy those cigarettes," the clerk said.

"Any strangers who've bought them recently?" Mary asked.

"Yeah, there's one stranger who came into town a week or two ago who bought them a few times."

Mary's heartbeat quickened. "Do you know where he is?"

"Right now? No. How should I know? He just comes in here to buy kreteks."

"Have you seen him around town at all?"

The clerk tugged at the silver earring studs dotting his left earlobe. "Not around town. But I saw him on the pier."

"You did?" Mary asked. "Where?"

"The far walkway. By the *Reliance*."

Mary wasn't sure where that was, but she could find out. "When did you see him there?"

"I dunno, on and off the past couple of days. My dad's fishing boat is moored a little ways down, so I saw him only from a distance, you know?"

"Have you seen him anywhere else?" Mary asked.

"Nope. Just at the pier."

Mary nodded to him. "Thanks."

The clerk just gave a one-shoulder shrug and went back to slouching on a stool behind the counter.

As she walked away from Barnaby's, Mary was suddenly hailed by a familiar voice. She saw Henry heading her way.

"Hi, Henry," she said.

"Hello." He glanced at the cigarette shop. "I saw you enter Barnaby's but thought my eyes were deceiving me."

"I wasn't buying cigarettes, but I was trying to get some information. Henry, do you know where the *Reliance* is?"

"Sure. The *Reliance* is a large ship on the far end of the docks. Why?"

"I think"—she bit her lip—"I think it might have to do with the bank robbery."

"Then let's go."

They went to the docks and down the walkways, passing fishing boats and yachts and speedboats all moored in their assigned berths. Mary confessed to Henry about Sandra's brother, his possible role in the bank robbery, and the kretek cigarettes he smoked. "I can't help thinking that Jesse hid Steve away somewhere, and now that I know he was hanging around this area of the docks, I wonder if maybe he put him on a boat."

Finally, they approached a magnificent yacht painted with flashy black and red stripes and the name *Reliance* in gold-scroll lettering on the side.

"Now what?" Henry asked.

"It might be a long shot, but that brand of kretek cigarettes has a distinctive gold, green, and blue pattern on the paper. I remember seeing it when I looked it up online, so the stub would have those colors too."

"So we look for gold, green, and blue-colored cigarette butts."

"I just hope he didn't throw all his cigarettes into the ocean," Mary said.

They went down each walkway one by one, their eyes scanning the wooden planks and scouring each nook and corner for just one of those colorful cigarette butts. Some of the boats' owners were onboard, and a few called greetings to Henry.

"Henry." A hearty voice hailed them from the top of a deep-sea fishing vessel. "Oh, hi, there, Mary."

Mary looked up and spotted Russell, Rebecca's husband, who was a fisherman. "Hi, Russell. I didn't realize this was where you moored your boat."

"Yep. What are you two doing? You look like you're on a scavenger hunt." Russell had a gruff voice, but his blue eyes were kind under his battered ball cap.

"Actually, we're looking for someone."

"You won't find him lurking under the pier," Russell joked.

"I wonder if you've seen him. He smokes clove cigarettes. The clerk at Barnaby's mentioned he'd seen him around this area in the past few days."

"Clove cigarettes?" Russell asked. "Those are the strange-smelling ones, right?"

Mary nodded. "We were looking for cigarette butts he might have dropped."

"Ah, I see, that's what you were doing. I saw someone smoking those cigarettes over there." He pointed to the next walkway. "Near *Holbrook's Hollow*. I remember because they smelled odd."

"Thanks, Russell."

"I might see you later today." Russell smiled, and his teeth shone white against his weathered face. "Because I got in this morning, I'm picking Ashley up from your store to take her to lunch."

"She might still be on her ice-cream diet."

"Yeah, Rebecca told me about the chipped tooth."

Mary waved good-bye to Russell, who went back to his work, and she and Henry headed to the next walkway. They spotted *Holbrook's Hollow* right away, a large deep-sea fishing boat with the name in bright-yellow block letters on the side.

"That's Jonas's boat," Henry said. "He broke his leg three weeks ago and hasn't been fishing since."

Holbrook's Hollow was moored only two berths from the end of the walkway. On one side was *Wicked Wager* and on the other side was the *Redemption*, while across the walkway was the *Chadbourne Luck* and *Lady's Revenge*.

Even as they approached *Holbrook's Hollow*, Mary thought she smelled the distinctive sweet scent of clove cigarettes, but with the breeze coming from the ocean, she couldn't be sure. She focused her eyes on the wooden planks of the walkway and searched the bases of the pillars for signs of the gold, green, and blue cigarette stubs.

"Mary," Henry said.

She looked up and saw him pointing to something at the base of a pillar next to the *Redemption*. When she approached, she saw two little stubs in the familiar gold, green, and blue pattern.

They both looked up at the *Redemption*. It was a smallish boat, with the curtains pulled over the small windows along the sides.

"I think I know who owns this," Henry said. "I think it's the Tyndalls. They go to Florida to see their grandkids at this time of year, so no one's been on the boat for a while."

"It would be perfect for someone to hide out." Mary had lowered her voice to almost a whisper. "Do you think Jesse is on board right now?"

"If he is, he's lying low. I don't hear anyone stirring inside."

Mary's heart raced as she and Henry cautiously boarded the *Redemption*. She was glad for Henry's presence, now that she was faced with the possibility of bumping into Jesse. If she'd been by herself, she'd have been forced to call dock security first, the more prudent option, rather than following her sense of urgency to try to find Steve.

Before approaching the door to the boat, she looked in the windows but couldn't see anything because the curtains were closed. She and Henry both paused, listening intently for any movement inside.

"Do you hear anything?" she whispered.

"No."

Henry looked at the door handle into the main cabin and frowned. "This door lock has been tampered with." He quietly grabbed the door handle and pushed on it, but it didn't budge.

"I don't think it's locked," Henry said. "I think it's just jammed because the lock was broken." He leaned harder on the door handle, and it rattled slightly.

They both froze, but there was still no sound from inside the boat.

"If Jesse were in there, I think he'd have either attacked us or tried to escape," Mary said in a low voice.

"I agree."

Henry slammed his weight against the door, and it opened with a sudden groan of wood and metal. Mary peered cautiously inside. The door opened into a tiny eating area, and there was a door leading from this front room deeper into the boat.

"Steve?" Mary called tentatively.

There was an answering muffled shout, and then the sounds of someone thrashing around, kicking at the sides of the boat. Mary and Henry hesitated, startled by the sudden sounds as they continued for several seconds. Then Mary headed toward the door on the other side of the room and pulled it open.

Steve Althorpe lay on the floor, his mouth gagged with a dirty strip of cloth, his hands and feet tied behind his back with rope and tethered to a metal hook in the wall.

He stared up at them with relieved eyes.

"Steve!" Mary rushed to him. She struggled to undo the tight gag over his mouth, but she broke a fingernail scrabbling at it. Henry knelt next to her and pulled out his pocketknife, slicing through the fabric.

Steve gasped. "Mary! How did you find me?"

"It's a long story," she said with a laugh, "but you're all right now."

"That man could come back...."

"I'll call dock security—I know the number of the guard-house—and the police right now." Henry rose and pulled out his cell phone.

Mary grabbed Henry's knife and sawed at the ropes tying Steve's wrists to the metal ring set in the wall near the floor. "I'm so relieved you're all right. I've been so worried and confused."

"Confused?" Steve asked her.

"You disappeared, and the police think you robbed the bank," Mary explained. "But I couldn't believe you'd do something like that."

"I'm glad you think so," Steve said.

"If I hadn't, I wouldn't have tried to find out where you were."

Mary cut through the ropes, and Steve sat up, rubbing his wrists, just as Henry returned from making his phone calls. "I called dock security; my friend Merrick's on duty today. He's going to call the police and lead them here to the boat when they arrive at the docks. He'll also keep an eye out in case Jesse comes back." He took the knife from Mary and worked on the ropes tying Steve's ankles together.

"What happened?" Mary asked Steve.

"I was at the back of the bank, about to dress for the reenactment, when someone knocked me out," Steve said. "I came to on the floor of this boat, but I wasn't tied to that ring in the wall—just my hands were tied. I heard a man talking on a cell phone just outside, so I got to my feet and looked out through a crack in the curtain. He was talking to a man named Vinny about getting a boat scrubbed of identification and a new ID put in place so he could take it and escape."

Henry looked grim. "I know Vinny. He's a 'boat restorer' in a neighboring town who's rumored to have some shady connections."

"It took me a while to realize he was talking about *my* boat," Steve said.

"It makes sense. Your boat is large and suited for a longer sea voyage," Mary said. "It would be a good boat to escape in. That also explains why the police can't find it."

"There." Henry finished with the rope, and Steve's ankles were free. They helped him to his feet, but he was shaky and leaned heavily on Henry. "Easy," Henry said.

"The man didn't let me stand up much in the past few days," Steve explained, gritting his teeth against the pain in his legs.

"He fed you?" Mary pointed to a seat. "Here, let's sit you down again." They walked Steve a few steps so he could sit down.

Steve said, "He's been coming a few times a day to give me food and water. He always has a mask on—the one I was going to use for the reenactment. But he didn't know that I'd already seen his face."

"You mean, that first day when he was on the phone?" Mary asked.

Steve nodded. "His face wasn't covered, and he didn't know I peeked through the window to see him. I had dropped back down to the floor by the time he finished his call and came inside."

"Did he ever say anything?"

"No," he said. "He spoke only once, and that was to promise me that he'd let me go just before he left town. And then he admitted he was keeping me hidden while the police investigated me for the robbery. That got me pretty upset, I can tell you."

"I'll bet," Mary said.

"But today, when he came to feed me, his cell phone rang and he answered it. He immediately headed out of the cabin to speak to whoever it was, but I could just barely hear a man's voice in the phone say, 'It's done.'"

Mary grew cold. "He must mean the boat is done. He might leave today."

"The police know about Vinny's side business," Henry said. "They just haven't been able to catch him in anything underhanded. If Steve's boat is at Vinny's place, they'll be able to intercept it before Jesse can get away."

"But they don't know yet that Vinny's altering Steve's boat." Mary pulled out her cell phone. "I'm going to call the police too."

She called 911, but she insisted on speaking to Chief McArthur.

"Chief McArthur is not available," the dispatcher said.

"You have to connect me to him. We know where the robber is, and he's going to escape today if the police don't get there in time."

The dispatcher hesitated, then said, "Hold please."

In a few minutes, Chief McArthur came on the line. "Mary?" There was a lot of ambient noise on his end of the phone. He must be outside speaking on a cell phone rather than in his office.

"Chief, we found Steve Althorpe tied up on a boat here at the docks."

"Yes, I know. The dispatcher told me about the 911 call the dock security officer called in. We'll have an officer on his way to you as soon as possible. We were pulled down the coast on a lead today, so we're a little shorthanded."

"We've been talking to Steve, and he overheard the robber talking to a man named Vinny who does reidentification of boats."

"I know what Vinny does," Chief McArthur said in a growling voice.

"Vinny finished putting a new identification on Steve's boat," Mary said. "The robber might take the boat and leave today if you don't stop him."

"All right, Mary, this is what I want you to do. Stay with Steve. We'll send an officer as soon as we can, but in the meantime, we'll look into Vinny. If the officer doesn't get there soon, don't worry."

Mary was relieved they were going to check out Vinny's place. She hoped they'd catch Jesse before he had a chance to take Steve's boat. "Thank you, Chief." She hung up.

She told Henry and Steve, "They're sending someone as soon as possible, but they're shorthanded today because they had a lead somewhere down the coast, and so they're all away from Ivy Bay."

"That's bad timing," Henry said.

"But maybe it's good, because Chief McArthur is sending them to Vinny's place. They might be closer than they'd have been if they were here."

"Let's hope so," Steve said. "I wish I'd been able to get someone's attention before this. Even though I was tied up, I kept kicking the sides of the boat, hoping to at least get someone to call the dock security guard to investigate."

"No, there isn't anyone here who would have heard you," Henry said. "When I called Merrick and told him about finding you here on the *Redemption*, he told me the *Wicked Wager* and the *Chadbourne Luck* are owned by people who live down south and only come to Ivy Bay for the summer. *Lady's Revenge* is owned by a man whose family is out of town on vacation this week, and I already knew that *Holbrook's Hollow* is owned by Jonas, who broke his leg, so he wouldn't have gone near his boat."

"Jesse might have noticed that the boats on this end of the dock didn't have a lot of traffic," Mary said. "It might be why he chose to tie you inside the *Redemption*."

While they waited for the officer to arrive, Mary pulled back all the curtains to let light into the small room, and her eyes fell on the rope that had been tied around Steve's wrists. The rope for his wrists was different than the rope around his ankles. The rope around his wrists looked strangely familiar. Mary picked it up.

"This is Jayne's linen rope," she said before she could stop herself.

Steve eyed the rope and groaned. "Yes, I know."

"What do you mean, you know?"

"I knew that Sandra had asked Jayne for her rope. I think she was going to use it for something, but I stole it out of her purse. I was going to surprise Sandra by tying her up at the reenactment, kind of as a practical joke. I had the rope with me behind the bank, but when I came to in this boat, I saw that the robber had used my own rope to tie me up."

So that was how the linen fibers had gotten behind the bank.

"I've been chafing at that rope around my wrists for three days, wishing I'd never taken it," Steve said glumly.

Mary and Henry sat beside Steve for a while. Mary kept looking around at the boat. "Steve, did you see any bags? Did Jesse leave the loot from the safe-deposit boxes?"

Steve shook his head. "I didn't see anything like that, but I was only here in this room."

"Let's look," Mary said to Henry.

They spent the next half hour searching the boat, but they couldn't find the bags of valuables that Jesse had taken from the bank. By the time they had given up, they saw Deputy Wadell and a paramedic hurrying down the walkway, led by a heavyset dock security guard, whom Henry greeted as Merrick. Mary breathed a sigh of relief.

The paramedic immediately went to Steve in order to check him out. Deputy Wadell stood to one side, waiting, so Mary approached him. "Did Chief McArthur find Vinny?"

Deputy Wadell hesitated, as if wondering if he ought to tell her or not.

"I did call in to tell him about Vinny," Mary reminded him.

The deputy sighed and rolled his eyes, making him look even younger than his twentysomething years. But he answered, "Yes. They raided Vinny's shop, and last I heard, they found Mr. Althorpe's boat and arrested Vinny, but they didn't find Jesse Rink."

Mary's heart sank. "But where could he be? Would he come back here?"

"He'd probably go get the stuff he stole. It wasn't on Mr. Althorpe's boat."

The paramedic finally finished checking Steve over to make sure he was all right, then stepped back and nodded to Deputy Wadell. The deputy sat next to Steve and began taking his statement.

Mary sat nearby, listening. The deputy asked more questions, writing the answers down in his notebook. It took a long time, but soon Deputy Wadell seemed to be winding up.

Steve's eyes had begun to glaze over—so had Mary's and Henry's, for that matter—when he suddenly blinked and focused his attention out one of the side windows. His face grew hard and frantic. "That's him!"

Deputy Wadell looked out the window, following Steve's gaze. "Who?"

"The guy who kidnapped me."

Mary ran to one of the other windows and peered out. A familiar-looking man was climbing onto *Holbrook's Hollow*, which was moored next to the *Redemption*. He was the same dark-haired, squat man whom she'd seen at the pharmacy. He moved quickly and furtively, glancing around at the walkways as if he were afraid he was being followed. "It is Jesse," she whispered.

"Get away from the window," Deputy Wadell ordered her, and she pulled back. She saw that both Deputy Wadell and Deputy Merrick had drawn their guns. They silently left the cabin.

Henry was suddenly at her side, pulling her to the far side of the cabin. "Get down," he whispered.

Mary lowered herself to the floor, while Henry helped Steve to the floor also.

There was a shout: "Police! Put your hands on your head!" Mary recognized Deputy Wadell's voice. Then more shouting that she couldn't understand. She squeezed her eyes shut as she lay on the floor.

Then it was over. Henry crept up to a window to look out, and satisfied with what he saw, he helped Steve to sit up again. "It's all right, Mary. They got him."

She released a long breath and got to her feet. She hurried out of the cabin and off the boat to see Deputy Wadell forcing a handcuffed Jesse to sit on a locker at the base of a pillar in front of *Holbrook's Hollow.* Deputy Wadell then used his radio to call in that he'd captured Jesse Rink.

Henry stood beside her, and he put a comforting arm around her. "Are you all right?"

"Now I am." She let out another breath. "Oh, Henry, he could have come to the *Redemption.*"

"No, I think he was taking *Holbrook's Hollow* on purpose. It's a larger boat that he can take farther out into open water and escape. He wouldn't have expected anyone to notice it was missing until much later."

Deputy Wadell finished talking to the dispatcher and walked over to Mary. "Are you all right, Mrs. Fisher?"

"I'm fine." She gave a small laugh. "I thought you had to read him his Miranda rights."

The deputy grinned. "You've been watching too many crime shows. You only read someone's rights just before you ask them any questions."

"Does that mean I can't ask him any questions?"

Deputy Wadell gave her an exasperated look. "No, Mrs. Fisher, you can't ask him any questions."

Mary gave him a wistful look.

Finally, Deputy Wadell gave in. "All right, all right. I'll talk to Chief McArthur and make sure he tells you what happened."

"I'll hold you to that, young man. After all, you owe me."

"I do?"

Mary gave him a smug smile. "If it weren't for me, you wouldn't have gotten credit for the most dramatic arrest of the month."

NINETEEN

◆◆◆

The next morning, Mary was outside picking up the newspaper when she saw her neighbor Owen Cooper jogging. He saw her and waved, but instead of continuing on his morning run, he came up to her.

"Good morning, Owen," Mary said.

"Good morning." A smile like sunlight lit up his face. "I've got some great news that I just can't keep to myself."

"Then tell me. Don't keep me in suspense."

"I know you've been concerned about the bank for the past few weeks, and I haven't been able to say much, but I just got word this morning that Ivy Bay Bank & Trust is going to remain open."

"Oh, Owen, that's wonderful!" Mary clasped her hands to her chest.

"You might have seen a stranger in a suit at the bank the past few days," Owen said. "He was Justin Fairchild, and he was sent by the Neels Banking Group to evaluate the bank's finances. After going over the books, he confirmed that we're doing so well that there's no question of us closing."

"I could wish Mr. Fairchild had better timing," Mary said. "He arrived the day after the robbery."

Owen winced. "It couldn't be helped, but it was to Mr. Fairchild's credit that he didn't let it bias his assessment of the bank. And I heard that you found Steve tied up on a boat in the marina."

"But it was the police who nabbed the real bank robber." They chatted about the events of yesterday, which had appeared in the morning paper.

"I'd better finish my run," Owen finally said.

"The news about the bank is wonderful, Owen. I can't wait to tell Betty."

"See you later, Mary." Owen jogged off with a little extra kick in his step.

Mary sailed into the house and told Betty the good news.

"Thank the Lord!" Betty beamed at Mary. "Eleanor will be so pleased."

"I think everyone in town will be pleased."

When Mary went to open the store, she was hailed across the street by Jayne Tucker, who had just opened up Gems and Antiques. Mary hastily unlocked the front door, let Gus out of his carrier into the store, then closed the door and crossed the street to Jayne's storefront.

"Oh, Mary, did you hear? The bank's not going to close."

"I did. It's marvelous."

"And they found my deposit too!" Jayne's face shone with joy. "I'm so relieved."

"I'm so glad, Jayne."

"And I talked with Rich last night." There was only a hint of regret in Jayne's tone as she continued, "It's unfortunate, but he made me realize that sometimes unfair things happen, and we just have to let them go. If I hold on to my resentment and worry, it'll only make things worse."

Mary reached out to touch Jayne's hand. "That's very wise of you."

"I hired a private investigator to try to find the seller," Jayne said. "Rich didn't know about it, which made me feel even more guilty. I told him about it last night. We've decided that if the private investigator hasn't found anything by the end of the month, we're just going to let it go. It's not worth the extra expense to find the crooked seller who sold me the clock." A militant gleam came into her eyes as she added, "But if I ever see him again, I'll be sure to report him to the police right away."

Mary saw Rebecca approaching the bookstore and said good-bye to Jayne so she could hurry across the street.

"Did you hear?" Rebecca said.

"Yes, the bank's going to stay open."

Rebecca's brows knit. "It is?"

Mary paused as she swung open the door. "You didn't know?"

"I was going to ask you if you'd heard that they caught the man who robbed the bank."

The two of them looked at each other for a moment, then shared a laugh.

Mary put her purse away behind the counter. "How did you hear about the arrest?"

"Russell, of course."

"That's right; he was on his boat."

"He tried to take credit for you finding Steve because he pointed you in the right direction."

Mary laughed. "I guess he did. But how did he find out about what happened after that?"

"Oh, he talked to Deputy Wadell and got it out of him. It wasn't hard—the deputy was pretty proud of his arrest."

"Is he with Ashley today?"

"Yep. She's being spoiled by her daddy today."

Curiously, throughout the morning, Mary noticed several people heading down Main Street toward the bank, much more than normal, and there didn't seem to be anyone coming out of the bank.

"What's going on at the bank?" Rebecca asked, peering out the front window.

"I thought it was just my imagination, but if you're noticing it too...," Mary said.

Mary would have liked to leave Rebecca in charge so she could go to the bank to see what was going on, but there was a package delivery that morning, and soon the two of them were processing the new books that had arrived. Between the new books and the customers that came to the shop, they were kept busy all morning. Mary stopped only briefly when Megan came by on her bicycle.

Megan entered the store. "Did you hear? They caught the robber!"

Mary had to smile at her enthusiasm. "Yes, I heard. And Steve Althorpe is all right too."

Megan rummaged in her backpack. "I brought that new RAM stick for your computer. I can install it for you right now, if you want."

"Would you? That would be wonderful." Mary got out her laptop, glad she'd thought to bring it to work today. She had only done it because she was expecting a shipment of books and an extra computer was always handy when doing the book inventory.

In a few minutes, Megan had inserted the little metal rectangle into a small compartment on the back side of the laptop. "There. All done."

"How much do I owe you for the RAM stick?" Mary asked.

"No, don't worry about it. Bryan gave it to me for your computer. He has plenty of extras lying around, and he doesn't mind."

Mary made a mental note to give Megan a book later as thanks.

She remembered what Megan had said about her friendship with Bryan and the other kids in her computer club, and her fears about finding a place to belong. "How are things with you and Bryan? Are they still the same?"

"Well, when I went to his house to get the RAM stick, he asked why I hadn't been at computer club at school lately, so I told him."

"Does he do any of that hacking you were talking about?"

"Uh"—Megan bit her lip—"sometimes. But when I told him I didn't think it was right, he kinda said that he knew it was wrong. He'd only done it because some of the other guys were doing it. And then he said he admired me for standing against it."

Mary reached out to touch Megan's face. "You're very brave for standing up for what you think is right, and Bryan is a good guy for seeing that."

Megan ducked her head and mumbled, "Thanks, Mrs. Fisher."

Mary remembered her conversation with Bea. "Did your grandma talk to you in the past day or so?"

Megan's eyes suddenly lit with excitement. "Yeah! She talked to Mom and Dad last night. She said you came up with the idea for me to do some freelance computer work. That's awesome!"

"Well, try to contain your excitement," Mary teased. "What did your parents say?"

"They were all for it! Dad even says he knows a few small companies who might want to hire me hourly for IT support."

Mary had a vague notion that IT support had something to do with fixing computers. "Sounds exciting."

"Totally! I'll get to work on computers and actually get *paid* for it!"

Mary suppressed a smile. "What? You mean you wouldn't rather be working for minimum wage at a fast-food restaurant?"

Megan rolled her eyes. "Yeah, sure, Mrs. Fisher." But then she grinned. "I'd better go. I have to help Mom make lunch. See ya!"

Mary hoped everything would work out for this new opportunity for Megan. She seemed really happy about it, and it seemed to have boosted her confidence already.

Mary and Rebecca worked steadily until it was time for her lunch break.

"I think I'll head over to the bank," Rebecca said. "The crowd seems to have died down, but there's still some activity going on."

"Let me know what you find out," Mary said.

Mary worked on her own for an hour. Then Rebecca came rushing into the shop.

"You should go to the bank, Mary. Steve is back!"

"Today? But shouldn't he be home, resting?"

"He says he got a clean bill of health from the doctor, and he was too bored at home, so he came in to work today. People have been coming by the bank to talk to him."

Mary hurried to the bank, and Steve was indeed there. It was obvious that he was trying to work, but people kept crowding around him, asking what had happened to him and if he was all right.

Owen, still glowing at the news the bank was going to remain open, took Steve's popularity in stride. He watched indulgently as Steve sat at the lead banker's desk and talked to people.

Sandra was standing at her position behind the counter with no customers for her to serve. Mary smiled and walked over.

"How are you doing?" Mary asked.

Sandra tilted her head to the side. "I'm all right, I suppose." But her face was more relaxed than it had been all week, which eased Mary's worry about her.

"Is Jesse all right?" Mary asked in a low voice.

Sandra said sadly, "The police are still talking to him, but they found out the gist of what happened and told me about it."

Mary studied Sandra's face. "You shouldn't blame yourself for any of this. You had a very difficult decision to make."

"I know, but I can't help second-guessing everything I did since he came into town."

"He's your brother. What else could you do?"

"Well, I knew he had probably been doing something illegal in Boston and was running from the law. I could have refused to let him stay with me."

"No, that isn't you. You would never do that."

"It might have prevented him from discovering about the reenactment and deciding to steal the money. He confessed that he couldn't resist because it seemed like an easy opportunity to get some cash fast and escape."

"I can see why he thought that." Especially in a trusting, close-knit town like Ivy Bay.

Sandra said, "Did you know he didn't originally plan for Steve to look like the prime suspect in the robbery? After the robbery, he was going to take Steve's boat and escape, but then he belatedly realized that the police would be looking for it, thinking Steve was trying to get away with the robbery loot. So he found out about Vinny and hired him to change the boat's ID."

"I see. That's why he kept Steve tied up on the boat. He couldn't have Steve escaping, and he needed the police to suspect Steve until the boat was done."

Sandra nodded. "There's one thing I'm glad about. Jesse could have just killed Steve, but he didn't want to do that. That's why he kidnapped him instead, hid him on the *Redemption*, and gave him food and water every day."

"But you also asked him not to hurt Steve, and you made him promise that Steve would be all right. It shows that he loves you."

Sandra looked thoughtful for a long moment. "I suppose so," she said slowly. "The police told me that when they were questioning Jesse, he insisted that I knew absolutely nothing about the robbery and was completely innocent."

"He was trying to protect you, despite the trouble he'd caused."

Sandra blinked, surprised by what Mary had said. "I never thought of it that way."

"Did the police find what he stole from the safe-deposit boxes?"

"Yes. It was on *Holbrook's Hollow*."

Now Mary understood. "So when he was trying to escape, he didn't pick that boat at random."

"Not at all. When the police raided Vinny's place, Jesse had been there, but he escaped. Since he was familiar with the Ivy Bay docks and he thought no one in Ivy Bay would know him, he went back to recover the stolen valuables from *Holbrook's Hollow*. He didn't purposely put it on *Holbrook's Hollow* because he was going to escape in the boat, but he obviously wouldn't put it on the *Redemption* with Steve."

"There's one thing I wanted to ask you. Were you at the root cellar?"

Sandra was startled. "How did you know?"

Mary reached into her purse and took out the earring, sliding it across the counter toward her.

Sandra colored. "Yes. After the robbery, I remembered about the book Steve had lent to me. He'd been so excited about the robbery that he'd even gone to the county clerk's office to find the original root cellar where the robber hid to escape the sheriff in 1870, and he told me where it was. But I remembered that Jesse had been hiding in my bedroom when Steve came over to lend me the book, and Jesse overheard

Steve telling me about the shanty and the root cellar by the oak tree. When Steve disappeared, I wondered if maybe Jesse hid out in the same root cellar that Elias Cowper did, so I went there and found the cellar, but he wasn't there."

That's why she hadn't gone farther in the cellar—she'd only been looking to see if Jesse and Steve were there.

Something over Mary's shoulder caught Sandra's attention, and a mischievous twinkle appeared in her eyes. "Ooh, Mr. Cooper has another one."

Mary turned and saw Judith Dougher's improbably yellow hair as she entered the bank. She looked rather sheepish as she hesitated, seeing the crowd around Steve.

"What do you mean?" Mary asked Sandra.

"After the robbery, a bunch of people pulled their accounts from the bank. But all morning, they've all been coming in to reinstate their accounts. Steve's been too busy talking to people, so Mr. Cooper has been doing the accounts. I think he's feeling a bit vindicated." Sandra gestured toward the bank's president.

Owen did indeed seem rather pleased with himself as he beckoned to Judith. She sat in the chair across from him and looked a bit like a naughty schoolgirl in front of the headmaster.

Mary said to Sandra, "In his heart, Owen is happy to have people come back to the bank. They're like his family."

Sandra's eyes grew misty with unshed tears. "Mr. Cooper and Steve both forgave me."

"For what?"

"I confessed about hiding the petty-theft charge on my record when I applied to the bank. I explained that I'd gotten the charge because I was taking the blame for something my brother did, but I still shouldn't have hidden it from them. But they both were very kind and gracious to me."

"That sounds exactly like Steve and Owen."

"Steve said that he honored me for telling the police about my brother despite my love for him. He said that in the years I've been working at the bank, I've proven I'm an honest, good worker, and I don't have to worry about my job."

"Oh, Sandra, that's wonderful. You must be so relieved."

She smiled. "I am. It was breaking my heart to think I'd be fired and have to leave Ivy Bay."

The words struck a chord in Mary's heart. She understood exactly how Sandra felt about this wonderful town. The community felt like her family, which was why it had been so awful to think that anyone she knew had been involved in the robbery.

A customer came to the window, and Mary bid Sandra good-bye so she could serve him.

As Mary headed across the street, she could see the ocean in the distance over the tops of the storefronts and the roofs of the houses. The picture made her stop and drink it in.

In such a short time, Ivy Bay had become incredibly dear to her. It had truly become home. She understood how Sandra felt because she knew, deep in her heart, that Ivy Bay was where she belonged.

ABOUT THE AUTHOR

Camy Tang grew up in Hawaii and now lives in San Jose, California, with her engineer husband and rambunctious dog, Snickers. She graduated from Stanford University and worked as a biologist researcher for nine years, but now she writes full-time. She is a staff worker for her church youth group, and she leads one of the worship teams for Sunday service. On her blog, she ponders knitting, spinning wool, dogs, running, the never-ending diet, and other frivolous things. Camy loves hearing from readers. You can write to her at Camy Tang, PO Box 23143, San Jose, California 95153, and you can visit her on the Web at CamyTang.com.

A CONVERSATION WITH CAMY TANG

——◆◆◆——

Q: *What's your favorite vacation spot?*

A: My favorite trip was one to England for my fortieth birthday! I'd love to go back to look at the lovely manor houses and their grounds, as well as visit the incredibly old churches.

Q: *What was something interesting or important that you learned while researching and writing this novel?*

A: I especially loved researching about how books are constructed. It has inspired me to try my hand at making my own blank books for my prayer journals and also as gifts!

Q: *If you could go to Ivy Bay, which place/shop would you visit first?*

A: Mary's bookstore, of course! I love reading, especially cozy mysteries. I've been especially intrigued by books set during the First or Second World Wars. The time period is so interesting.

Q: *Do you have any pets? Have they ever helped you solve a mystery like Gus helps Mary?*

A: I have a wonderful dog named Snickers whom we rescued from a shelter, and she fills our days with joy. But instead of solving mysteries, she mostly sleeps all day.

Q: *Mary often goes to the library when sleuthing out a mystery. What's the library like in your hometown?*

A: I'm very fortunate to live near San Jose State University, and the libraries available to the public are big and beautiful and terrific for research.

Q: *What's your favorite type of book to read?*

A: I really enjoy historical books, especially books set in England. But I also read lots of other genres including contemporary romance, mystery and suspense, and young adult fiction.

Q: *Mary loves to snuggle up with a cup of tea or a quilt and read at the end of the day. How do you like to spend the quiet hours of an evening at home?*

A: I love to read, too! I have a cozy "book corner" in my home where I've set up a comfy chair with a table nearby for my teapot, teacup, honey, and milk. I also have a lovely footrest that my husband bought for me for Christmas. On a cold day, I like to snuggle under a pink fuzzy blanket that I crocheted myself.

PUMPKIN SPICE ICE CREAM

Be sure to freeze the inner container of your ice-cream maker the night before making this delicious, creamy ice cream.

> 2 cups heavy cream
> 1 cup whole milk
> 2 egg yolks
> ½ cup sugar
> 1 teaspoon vanilla extract
> 1½ cups canned pumpkin
> 1 teaspoon ground ginger
> 1 teaspoon ground cinnamon
> ¼ teaspoon salt
> ⅛ teaspoon ground cloves
> ½ cup maple chips or, if not available,
>   butterscotch chips
> ½ cup crushed graham crackers

Combine cream and milk in a saucepan over medium heat, and heat until the mixture almost boils, about five to eight minutes. In the meantime, whisk egg yolks, sugar, and vanilla extract in a small bowl until light yellow and smooth, about one to two minutes. Add four tablespoons of hot cream/milk to the egg yolk mixture and whisk. Gradually add the warmed egg yolk mixture to the hot cream/milk in a thin stream, constantly whisking to prevent the eggs from curdling.

Reduce heat to low and cook until slightly thickened enough to coat the back of a spoon, or about 170 degrees. Whisk in the pumpkin and spices until combined. Pour mixture into a bowl and cool in the fridge overnight, or you can chill it in an ice bath for thirty minutes.

Pour chilled mixture into freezer bowl of ice-cream maker and turn the machine on. Let it mix until the mixture thickens, about twenty-five minutes. During the last five minutes, add the chips and crushed graham crackers. Transfer the ice cream into a container and place in the freezer until firm, about two hours.

FROM THE GUIDEPOSTS ARCHIVE

- - ◆ ◆ - -

Who sings songs to a troubled heart. —Proverbs 25:20 (NAS)

My daughter Julie had joined Al-Anon to find out how to do what was best for her brother Jon. Her advice to me was of the variety "Let go and let God," "One day at a time" and "If you love him, don't help him." Her stern words didn't take away any of the agony of rejecting my son.

Then Jon's twin brother Jeremy called. "Mom, he keeps showing up here, begging to stay with me." I heard the pain in his troubled voice. Jennifer, my middle child, cried on the phone. "He's our flesh and blood!" Jon phoned occasionally himself, sometimes in a rage, other times gentle and funny.

In the midst of the turmoil, I searched for peace. Sitting in the brown recliner that Jon loved, I closed my eyes, listening hard for God's silent voice.

Gene had started leaving the radio on day and night. "It's for the cat," he explained, "so she doesn't get so lonely when we're out." Sure enough, we often came home to find her curled up by the radio. My heavy heart seemed to curl up there too:

Morning by morning, new mercies I see.
All I have needed Thy hand hath provided;
Great is Thy faithfulness, Lord, unto me!
(Thomas O. Chisholm, 1866–1960)

How faithful You remain, dear Lord, no matter how discouraged
I am. —Marion Bond West

A NOTE FROM THE EDITORS

We hope you enjoy Secrets of Mary's Bookshop, created by the Books and Inspirational Media Division of Guideposts, a nonprofit organization. In all of our books, magazines and outreach efforts, we aim to deliver inspiration and encouragement, help you grow in your faith, and celebrate God's love in every aspect of your daily life.

Thank you for making a difference with your purchase of this book, which helps fund our many outreach programs to the military, prisons, hospitals, nursing homes and schools. To learn more, visit GuidepostsFoundation.org.

We also maintain many useful and uplifting online resources. Visit Guideposts.org to read true stories of hope and inspiration, access OurPrayer network, sign up for free newsletters, download free e-books, join our Facebook community, and follow our stimulating blogs.

To learn about other Guideposts publications, including the best-selling devotional *Daily Guideposts*, go to ShopGuideposts.org, call (800) 932-2145 or write to Guideposts, PO Box 5815, Harlan, Iowa 51593.